A Book for Friends and Relatives
of a Divorcing Family

# Scenes *from a* Divorce

Neil Paylor
and
Barry Head

WINSTON PRESS

Cover design: Sharon Keegan

Library of Congress Catalog Card Number: 82-50292

ISBN: 0-86683-635-7

Printed in the United States of America.

5  4  3  2  1

Winston Press, Inc.
430 Oak Grove
Minneapolis, Minnesota 55403

To our own families
and the many, many others
who have found the courage to grow
through times that were hard

# CONTENTS

# FOREWORD

Growth seldom comes easily for any of us at any time of life. At Family Communications, our non-profit production company for our public television children's series, *Mister Rogers' Neighborhood,* we're most concerned about how young children grow. In fact, one of the descriptions of our work that I like best is that we try to provide "a place where friends help children find within themselves the courage to grow."

Our concern for young children means, naturally, that we are also concerned about the emotional health and well-being of their families. For it is in their families that children have the best chance to learn they are loved, capable of loving, and able to cope with the difficulties that growing brings.

But it is not only children who grow. Adults go on growing, and families grow, too. Even after a divorce, a family keeps growing—although it may look as if it's falling apart. A divorce doesn't mean that parents stop being parents or that children stop being sons and daughters, brothers and sisters, grandsons and granddaughters, nieces and nephews. The fact that friendships continue to grow as well, as this book points out, can make a lot of difference in how those other relationships develop through the anguish of a family breakup.

How best to be helpful is a recurring question in this book, as it is for all of us in real life. I very much like the way the book suggests that there is a lot we cannot expect to do, as well as a lot that we may be doing even when it seems we are doing very little. We cannot, for instance, expect to shorten people's grief or lessen people's anger.

We cannot expect to resolve their conflicting feelings, and we cannot heal their hurts for them. We can, on the other hand, do so much by simply being present and available, supportive and nonjudgmental, by offering a hand whether it's taken or not, or lending an ear when it's needed. That may not sound like much, but it is. By just being there, we can help our friends or loved ones to reaffirm their sense of self and self-value, two of the most important coping defenses for adults and children who are going through stressful times.

I know that the authors wanted *Scenes from a Divorce* to provoke both individual thoughts and group discussions. Although it is short and easy to read, their book has led me to lengthy and difficult reflection. Very little in it seems accidental. As I read the scene in which the young Lynch children are watching television, I found myself thinking once again how terribly important it is for adults to know what the children in their care are watching on television, and to be there to help them learn the difference between reality and fantasy. It's especially critical when children are bringing powerful "inner dramas" of their own to the programs they are watching.

I also found myself reflecting on the many practical problems of single parenting, and thinking how helpful it could be for newly single parents to talk with one another about the daily trials they face. And what a hard time grandparents have! They must try to work through their own feelings as parents of divorcing parents and at the same time be sensitive to the needs of their grandchildren. We sometimes forget that a divorce can be hard on grandparents, too.

If I had to name one thing that persons close to a divorcing family could do to help the children, it would be this: Let them know again and again that they are not responsible for the breakup of their family. And one more thing: Let them know that even when husbands and wives decide not to live together anymore, they can still go on being loving fathers and mothers.

I hope that *Scenes from a Divorce* will encourage readers to think and talk about more things that are likely to be both important and perplexing for all of us all our lives long—things like ambivalence, the meaning of loyalty, the relationship between anger and love, and the nature of compassion.

I have known Neil Paylor and Barry Head for several years, and they have worked closely with Family Communications. *Scenes from a Divorce* grew slowly from idea to realization. That's usually the way that things (and people) grow best. But such measured growth is not always possible. Divorce, for instance, forces people to stretch quickly to—and sometimes even beyond—their limits.

I hope that this book will help those who are experiencing even the most difficult times. I believe it will.

FRED M. ROGERS

Creator and host of *Mister Rogers' Neighborhood*

# INTRODUCTION

Sooner or later, you will go through a divorce. It may not be your own—and yet it may. More likely it will involve the splitting up of relatives or friends. These days, all of us can expect to have our lives touched and changed by the coming apart of a family we know. One reason we wrote this book was to acknowledge that the experience of divorce is painful and disruptive not only for husband, wife, and children but also for those close to them. We know that relatives and friends can be helpful at such a time—and generally want to be. We know that they can also feel helpless. And sometimes their efforts to help turn out even worse than no help at all.

A second reason we wrote this book was out of a particular concern for children and the impact of divorce upon them. It is often through children—theirs or ours—that we become enmeshed with a divorcing couple. When a husband and wife are breaking up, they work so hard to cope with their own feelings that they may be severely handicapped in meeting the emotional needs of their children. Therein lies an important opportunity for those of us on the edges.

What we offer here, then, is a book that is intended primarily for the relatives and friends of a divorcing family. It is not a definitive "how-to" book because there are certainly many, many ways for relatives and friends to be helpful. Moreover, each human being and each human relationship is unique, so there can be no single set of circumstances from which we can all derive answers. What we can find in a story like this one, though, are fresh insights into the dynamics of need and response. It may encourage us to think through the roles we may play, intentionally or inadvertently, in similar situations. We would like to think that this book might be useful in discussion groups, where it may prompt people to share their perceptions and concerns and discover the insights most valuable to them. For the individual reader, we hope it will provide some new ways to think about an old and eternally difficult problem—how best to help others.

We wish to acknowledge with great gratitude the contributions made to this book by two knowledgeable friends, John Hitchcock and Margaret McFarland. Dr. Hitchcock is a psychoanalyst in private practice in Pittsburgh. Dr. McFarland is a psychologist and chief consultant to Family Communications which, among other things, produces the landmark children's television series, *Mister Rogers' Neighborhood.* If this book proves helpful, it is largely due to their willingness to spend time with us and to speculate on the meaning of incomplete and imaginary people and events. We would also like to acknowledge the creative contribution of a writer colleague, David Forthuber, whose imagination and deft pen helped budge us off dead center when we needed it, and the very creative and constructive suggestions of our editor, Pamela Espeland. We are deeply grateful, too, to Elaine Lynch, Margaret Fuller, and Sally Decker for their patient manuscript preparation. Finally, to the Lilly Endowment, whose generous grant to Family Communications brought this book into being, we give our very special thanks.

A book can initiate new relationships or deepen familiar ones. Writing this one has meant both for us. We hope that reading and using it will mean the same for you.

# Scenes from a Divorce

# THE MAIN CHARACTERS*

WILL MORGAN

The narrator; the pastor of Sixth Presbyterian Church in Pittsburgh, he presided over the marriage of Fred and Karen Lynch

FRED and
KAREN LYNCH

A young couple undergoing a separation and divorce after nine years of marriage

NATHAN and
SHARON LYNCH

The Lynches' seven-year-old son and five-year-old daughter

BILL and
VIRGINIA SAWYER

Karen Lynch's parents

DWIGHT and
RUTH LYNCH

Fred Lynch's parents

DR. ABRAHAM LEWI

Will's friend; a psychiatrist

JACK and
DIANE GEARY

Friends of Fred and Karen Lynch; they have a daughter, Jennifer

GLORIA HOUCK

Fred Lynch's sister

NANCY QUINN

A babysitter for the Lynch children

*Note: The characters portrayed in this book are fictional and are not intended to resemble any living persons.

# PROLOGUE

When I pronounced Fred Lynch and Karen Sawyer husband and wife nine years ago, I and most of us who knew them thought it was a good match. I'd known Karen since high school—I was a senior while she was a freshman. Her parents, Virginia and Bill Sawyer, were regular customers at my father's pharmacy until he retired. When I came home from seminary, I met Fred, who complemented Karen's reserve with his outgoing good humor. Theirs was the first marriage ceremony I ever performed, and it came just after I had accepted a call to be the pastor of the Sixth Presbyterian Church here in Pittsburgh. In the years that followed, I baptized both their children—Nathan Emory and Sharon Sawyer Lynch. When Karen and Fred divorced last year, no one understood why, myself included.

In all, then, I'd known Karen for about fifteen years, but of course that didn't mean much in terms of really getting to know her. During the final year of her marriage to Fred, I hadn't spent more than a total of two hours with her and her family. They had never actually joined Sixth Church, and I don't think they were even regular churchgoers. For my part, I had my hands full with the lives of my parishioners.

I'd been much closer to the two of them at the time of their engagement. In those days I'd stop in for supper at either Karen's or Fred's parents' house every few weeks, and conversation would flow easily and range widely. Karen and Fred came from very different backgrounds, but that seemed an asset then. Karen's family had money; Fred's folks were farm people. I remember Karen saying that sometimes she felt more at home with the Lynches than with her own parents. She'd been eager to get away from home after high school but balked at going to the university in the East which her mother and father championed. She chose a local college instead—far enough away but not too far. That's where she met Fred.

Fred was a bright fellow, but he had a lot of trouble deciding what he wanted to do with his life. He'd thought about farming, but his father discouraged him, saying that nowadays the work was too demanding and the rewards too meager. The police chief in the community where the Lynches lived was a close family friend, and it was he who suggested to Fred that police work might make a challenging profession. For some reason the notion stuck. Fred's father urged him to go to college to see whether he had other interests, and the police chief agreed it was a good idea: A college education, he pointed out, would give him an edge for advancement. So Fred went off to college.

It wasn't at all what he'd expected. After two years he was fed up with what he called the "rah-rah antics" of his contemporaries. He'd already met Karen by then, and he felt ready to get going in the real world. For him, this seemed to mean marrying, working, and settling down. He quit school and joined the force as a plain old cop on a beat. Soon after that they came to me to get married.

I think Fred would have been happy if Karen had agreed to have children right away and simply settled into routine domesticity. That wasn't at all what she had in mind, though. Not only did she want to finish college, but she talked about going on for a graduate degree, too—an M.A. in Art History. After that, she thought, she might consider teaching. They compromised: Karen finished college, Fred got his happy home, and they both promised to think about the rest.

Looking back at it now, it seems as if those first four or five years together were their best. They didn't have any money to speak of, but they were both interested in what they were doing and interested in each other. I know that Karen's father helped her out a little bit now and then, but

I don't think Fred ever knew about it. Perhaps it was better that he didn't; it would have been hard on his pride. They lived very carefully, and I remember the great satisfaction Fred expressed when somehow they had scraped together enough money to make a down payment on a modest home of their own.

I saw less of them after that. Then one day, all of a sudden, Nathan and Sharon were five and three. I do recall bumping into Karen somewhere along about then and being pleased that she hadn't given up her plans to go back to school. Karen mentioned that Fred was fretting a bit about the slow pace of advancement in his job and didn't like the day-to-day life of a policeman in a large industrial city. There was nothing she said, though, that made me think there might be anything wrong between them. But just over a year ago I caught the rumor that they were "in trouble," and then someone told me they had separated.

The news upset me. When you marry a couple, you feel a lasting bond with them. In some way you've shaped their beginnings and helped them over an important crossing. Fred and Karen's wedding had helped me to get started with my ministry, and I was their friend as well as their pastor. I felt very reluctant to see the first couple I'd married get a divorce—for my sake as well as theirs.

I determined to see if there was any way I could help. There were some resources I could draw on—a year of clinical pastoral training at St. Elizabeth's hospital in Washington, D.C., and courses in human development and family counseling. So I had a start. Even so, I didn't know exactly where or how to begin. I don't think any of us do, we who are on the periphery of a family breakup. I don't just mean ministers or family counselors or others who are meant to be helpers by profession. I mean anyone— any relative or friend—who cares about the members of a family going through the anguish of a divorce. We all play roles whether we choose to or not, whether we wade into the fray or do nothing. Since we are all cast into our roles willy-nilly, it seems to me that we need to think very carefully in advance about what we want those roles to be. How else can we make reasoned decisions about how we should behave and the kinds of help we should offer?

But that's hindsight. To begin with, I was concerned far more about what I ought to *do* with that family than what I ought to *be* to them. It was bound to be a painful year for many people, and it was. Out of it, though, came growth— for Fred and Karen, Nathan and Sharon, Bill and Virginia Sawyer, Dwight and Ruth Lynch, and probably for everyone else whose lives were touched by that one divorce. For me, too, the year brought growth, along with a great deal of clarification and discovery.

It's the story of that growth that I want to relate here. Before I begin, though, I'd like to describe the visit Karen paid to me a few weeks ago, because it seems to bring the whole year's events full circle. Or perhaps I should say "full spiral," because nothing ever comes back exactly to where it began.

I knew from Karen's mother, Virginia Sawyer, that Karen was due in from Cincinnati for a few days, but I was surprised and pleased when she called and asked if she could stop by and say hello. The last time I had seen her was at her cousin's wedding, which I performed, and that had taken place six months or so ago, just before Karen moved away.

Karen seemed confident and at ease when she came in the door of my office at Sixth Church. We covered all the small-talk topics, like what single life was like in Cincinnati and how it felt to be back in school once more. She'd found it all a bit lonely and frightening for a while, she admitted, but she felt well settled now and was pleased with the city, her friends, and her life.

"How are Nat and Sharon doing?" I asked.

"I'm still not always sure what's going on with them," she replied. "The move was a difficult adjustment—that and being away from their grandparents and their father. I feel guilty about that sometimes, but I needed to be off on my own. They'll be here during the summer and they'll see everyone then for a good long spell. They're looking forward to that."

"I'll bet you'll welcome some time off, too."

She laughed. "I can't wait! Being a single parent really takes a lot out of you, but being tired sure beats being angry all the time."

"How do you think the divorce has affected the children?"

"They'll be marked by it, of course. But I've gotten over thinking they'll be permanently damaged. At least most days. Nathan likes his new school and is making friends. Sharon, at last, has stopped being as clingy as she was. For a while I thought she was really going to have problems. No, I'm pleased with the way they're getting along."

"It's amazing what we can all survive and even grow from," I said. "You know, I did some growing that year, too."

"How so?"

I told her how hesitant I had been at first about moving, uninvited, into her family's troubles. "I felt there was something I should do, but I really didn't know what it was," I explained. "I was very uncomfortable that first time I came to see you. Just after you and Fred had separated. Remember?"

She nodded. "No one knew what to do, Will. And let's face it, I was hard to approach. I was hurt . . . and embarrassed to admit that I had problems too large for me to handle alone. Yes, I remember that afternoon very well.

"What I remember best about that time is the exhaustion," she went on. "It was all I could do to put one foot in front of the other. What little energy I had went to the children. I don't think I had an ounce to spare."

"Or an ounce of hope, either. That's what I felt when I saw you. And I believe the two do go together."

"Maybe so. If I'd had any hope, I might have tried some counseling. I remember you suggested that."

"Looking back, do you think it would have made any difference?"

"I do think so. But not as a way to save our marriage," she quickly added. "That time had passed. It might have helped us face what happens when marriages don't get saved, though."

She paused to look at her watch. "Mom and Dad are expecting me for dinner, so I'm going to have to run," she said. "But I do want to tell you something before I go. Your visit was important to me, Will. You held out a hand. And even if I couldn't take it right then, you started me thinking that it might be okay to lean on other people's shoulders when I needed to . . . that they wouldn't mind. I guess I began to feel that I hadn't been kicked out of the human race after all."

"Here I thought I'd botched it—that I'd said all the wrong things." I smiled and stood up as she did. Karen held out her hand, and I took it for a moment.

"Say hello to your mom and dad for me, and tell your mom I hope to see her Sunday," I said.

"I'll do that." Then she was gone.

What she'd told me started me thinking again about that first time I'd gone to see her. I hadn't known what I would be walking into or how I would respond. I knew that I wanted to help, if I could, but I didn't know how I'd manage to do it, if at all. Would she resent my barging into her life? Because that's what I did—I didn't even call ahead to ask if I could come over. Maybe if I had I would have ended up simply talking to her on the telephone and thinking that was enough. And though this story may not have turned out any differently for Karen and Fred and their families, it would have for me.

# Scene One: May

The aliens had control of the Starship Enterprise. The crew, paralyzed by the force field, sat at their posts like statues. Only Captain Kirk could move and talk—and he was desperately trying to keep his mind from divulging the secrets of the Enterprise's energy system. But the telepathic interrogation was fierce....

"Are they really going to hurt him, Mommy?" asked five-year-old Sharon Lynch, leaning up close to her mother.

"No, honey, it's only pretend," Karen told her. "He's not really being hurt."

"They're only actors," said Nathan, seven, not taking his eyes off the screen. "They have to come back again tomorrow to make another program."

Karen Lynch smiled. Those were the same reassuring words she had used with Nathan when he was younger. She glanced over at him. He sat curled up tensely against the arm of the sofa, holding his blanket tightly against his cheek.

That grubby old blanket! she thought. Washing didn't help it; nothing helped it anymore. She remembered the tantrum he'd thrown when she told him it was time to get rid of it, how he'd flung himself on the floor screaming "It's mine! Gimme it back! It's mine!" Of course, as usual, he'd won in the end—but not before she'd exacted a promise that he wouldn't take it along when they went shopping or visiting in the future. "After all," she'd told him, "now *you're* the man of the household. You don't want people thinking you're still a little baby, do you?"

"You are a proud and stubborn man, Captain Kirk," droned the disembodied alien voice. "But you will tell us what we want to know." Kirk grimaced, straining against his bonds. He struggled to think of anything except the plans of the giant reactor he had once memorized so carefully. "Very well, then," said the voice. "You will have to come with us." And poof! Captain Kirk vanished from the starship's command console....

Sharon began to whimper. "Where'd he go, Mommy? Is he deaded?"

"No, honey, he's fine. You'll see. He'll be all right." The doorbell chimed. Karen got up with a sigh, unwinding Sharon from her arm. "Be back in a minute," she said.

As she passed the living room window, she saw that the visitor was Will Morgan from Sixth Church. In official uniform, too, she thought apprehensively, but then realized that it was only a white turtleneck under his dark raincoat.

She opened the door and smiled. "Hi, Will," she said. "Come on in."

"I'm not interrupting anything?"

"Heavens, no. And if you were, I'd probably be grateful! We're just watching TV. Coffee?"

"That'd be good. Thanks."

Will followed her into the kitchen, where the coffeepot sat ready on the warmer.

"I'm beginning to wonder if we're going to get any real spring this year," Will said. "It's sure a long time coming."

"I know. Sorry about the way things look," she said, gesturing around the kitchen. "I can't seem to keep up with everything. What I need is a wife."

He laughed, dismissing the disorder with a wave. "Good ones are hard to find these days."

She felt rebuked. "So are good husbands, it seems."

"I'm sorry. I didn't mean ...."

"I know, I know. I'm just edgy, that's all." She handed him his coffee. "What can I do for you?"

"Oh, nothing in particular," he said. "I was on my way over to see how Sally Carter was getting on with her hip and thought I'd look in. Of course, I'd be glad to see a little more of you and the kids every now and then...."

"Now you're going to make me feel guilty."

He shook his head. "It's not that at all."

They moved out of the kitchen to the round table in the adjoining alcove.

"I don't know what to tell you, Will, except that I find church so . . . so damned depressing these days. The last time I went I spent most of the service on the verge of tears. It was like bumping into an old friend who didn't recognize you anymore. I didn't feel like I belonged. In my new single state, I mean."

"Of course you belong. You know that. But I understand what you mean. Birth, marriage, even death—they're often easier for us than separation and divorce."

They stirred their coffee in silence for a moment.

"So how are things going?" Will asked.

Karen shrugged. "Not too bad, I guess, all in all. I'm worried about Sharon, though. She wanted to sleep with me again last night. She has nightmares. And something funny's going on between Nathan and his friends. They're not playing together the way they used to. I wish I could see inside their heads!"

"And Fred?"

"I don't really know. We talk about when he's to pick up the children and bring them back, but that's about all. The kids miss him, that's for sure, but they don't say much. One thing's certain: Separation hasn't gotten us anywhere. He'll file for divorce any day now."

"You and Fred still haven't tried counseling?"

She shook her head impatiently. "Too late. It wouldn't do any good. I'm not sure that either of us would even want it to do any good. He's set on his life, and I'm not going to give up mine. I think he's childish, and he thinks I'm spoiled. Our values are different. It's already been two years since we've been able to get through to each other.

Now I don't think either of us could even be bothered to really try. And yet . . . ."

"Yes?"

"And yet I never would have put us through all this pain. I mean, it's not just us and the kids. Look at poor Mom and Dad! And Fred's parents! Believe it or not, this will be the first divorce in either of their families for . . . for *ever*. It's something you just don't do, that's all. Fred's going ahead in the name of his own sweet happiness, never mind what anybody else is feeling . . . it's so selfish!"

"So you'd still be willing to go on. Together, I mean."

She nodded.

"Then don't you think you and Fred owe it to everyone to try counseling? I'd be glad to recommend two or three people . . . ."

"I don't know. Let me think about it," she said, feeling the tears rising. She reached up to wipe her eyes with the back of her hand. "Don't mind me. I do this all the time, and it makes me mad that I can't control it. I cried in the lawyer's office last week. Oh, it's so hard to talk about it, Will! I don't believe it's happening, my feelings are all out of control, I don't know what to say to the children . . . ." She took a deep, uneven breath and painstakingly secured a wisp of hair behind her ear. " . . . so I just try to stay busy, and watch television, and . . . I don't know, just sort of pretend to everyone that nothing's different."

"I'm sure the children know you're upset," Will said gently.

Karen nodded. "Sharon came into my room yesterday. I was crying, and she asked me why. I said someone I knew was very sick, and that made me sad. I didn't know what else to say. And I didn't trust myself to try to say anything sensible."

"What you did say summed up the situation pretty well, if you ask me. It can help, too, to talk with them about the simple things—who is going to live where, who will look after them, when they will see their father . . . things like that. And that it's okay to feel sad and cry. Or even to feel angry. Sometimes talk like that can help them ask you the questions they really need to have answered."

Sharon came trotting around the corner and headed for her mother's lap. "I didn't know where you had gone, Mommy," she complained. With her thumb in her mouth, she settled in against her mother's breast.

"I'm right here, honey," Karen said, rocking gently back and forth. "Right here."

"Hello, Sharon," Will said. "Maybe you remember me. We've met a couple of times at church."

Sharon nodded without looking at him. Will rose to leave.

"I'll be on my way," he said. "Don't get up. And call me, Karen, please, if you and Fred decide to keep on trying. There is help available out there, and you never know— it may not be too late even now."

"Okay. And thanks, Will, for coming by."

"'Bye, Sharon. Take care now," he said. He walked back through the living room and let himself out the door.

It was nice of him to come by, she thought, and he meant well. But there is no more "me and Fred." It's too late. Much too late.

I left Karen's house thinking I'd failed. What I wanted, I knew, was for Karen and Fred to stay together. If she didn't have any hope left that they could, and it seemed that she didn't, I wanted to give her that hope: *my* hope that the past could be salvaged. About the last thing I'd said to her was "call me if you and Fred decide to keep on trying." Maybe she'd take that to mean that she couldn't call me if they didn't.

It struck me then that what she needed was someone to give her hope for the present and the future. If I'd let go of *my* hope and focus instead on helping her to find her own . . . . I'd taken a first step by going to visit her. Now I wanted to take another. I was drawn to Karen and Fred and their children, and I felt the need to stay involved. But first I had to learn how to put my own disappointment aside, and there was someone who I was sure could get me started in that direction.

I'd known Dr. Abraham Lewi for only about a year, but from the moment we met at a dinner with mutual friends I was struck by this dapper, bald psychiatrist's evident compassion for human troubles and understanding of the breadth of human experience. Although we met from time to time on social occasions, the meetings I enjoyed the most took place in Schenley Park. We'd jog together in the late afternoon every couple of weeks and then walk back to Squirrel Hill, where we both lived. During those twenty minutes we'd talk about whatever was uppermost in our minds—the international situation, the economy, his golf game, the compatibility of religion and psychiatry, whether I should mate my Gordon Setter, Cindy (who often accompanied us), or the influence of Western values on our respective heritages. Abe was the only person I've met so far who could manage to look well-groomed even in a baggy grey sweatsuit.

I decided that during our next walk home I'd start using him as a sounding board for my relationship with Karen and, subsequently, anyone else in and around the Lynch and Sawyer families I might talk to. From the beginning, Abe was cautious in forming opinions.

"Whatever you tell me, Will," he said, "I can't know those people as you do. Without firsthand knowledge there's not much I can say about their particular case. It would just be speculation—and possibly very misleading speculation. Generalities . . . yes. I can make some of those. There sometimes seem to be patterns. But answers? Almost never. Whether whatever we talk about applies to your friends' case is something for you to decide—as is what use you make of it." He smiled. "But I do know *you* firsthand."

I told him how hesitant I felt about intruding on them while, at the same time, my status as minister and friend made me want to move forward. "What do you think I can do to be helpful, Abe?"

"Perhaps it's a question of expectations," he said. "What do you really expect to be able to do for them? That often puts professional caregivers like you and me into a real bind. By training, and probably by self-selection, we want to be somebody's right hand. We want to be able to control events in a meaningful way. Then, again and again, we get into situations where we feel we can't.

"I've known caregivers who suffered acute depression because of that feeling of helplessness," he went on. "Their depression rendered them less able to do what they might have been able to do in the way of helping. I think good caregivers have to come to terms with their own unrealistic expectations. It's hard. It really is. So you came away from your friend, Karen, feeling you hadn't done much. But you did take her two important gifts."

"Namely?"

"You brought her your friendship, and you brought her your willingness to listen. Very significant gifts."

"She mentioned a couple of times that she was worried about the children. She wondered what was going on in their heads. So did I."

"So do we all! Children's behavior is bound to change when their parents break up, and that's another source of anxiety for whomever is looking after them. For instance, they may regress—you know, go back to teddy bears and sucking blankets and bedwetting after that's all supposed to be over. Regression as a result of stress is normal rather than pathological. A child may need to step back for a while from new developmental tasks in order to cope with some immediate stress. It's generally temporary. But it can make parents worried and even angry. Or if the boy . . . what was his name?"

"Nathan."

"If Nathan is suddenly becoming aggressive in inappropriate ways that are upsetting to the school and the neighbors . . . why, I remember one eight-year-old who was sleeping under his bed at night with knives and guns! His whole family was in a state of panic. That boy was afraid of *himself*—afraid, unconsciously, because there was no one to keep his sexual fantasies under control. You see, he was at an age when he was just beginning to internalize his parents' values, and suddenly, through divorce, he was deprived of his father as the primary support—and restraint—for his growing masculinity. The boy was very angry because he felt unprotected.

"The mother came to see me. What did I find out she'd told the boy? She'd told him: 'Come on, Johnny, act your age. You're the man of the house now.' How burdensome for a small boy! It denies him his right to regress and feeds right into his fantasies that he could be ... was ... *is* the man of the house. Give him a sense of value and importance, by all means! Tell him: 'Johnny, you're a real comfort to me.' Anything like that would be fine.

"But I'm rambling on. In any case, I doubt that this type of discussion is what your friend needed from you. Or what she needs from any of her friends. Friends and relatives so often tend to back away from someone else's family crisis. You, on the other hand, moved toward her. Isn't that ministry? I think it is."

"Other people do tend to back away, don't they?" I agreed. "I don't think they realize how much they can do just by sticking in there, being supportive, and listening. It's almost as though there were a fear of contagion—that they'd somehow catch the divorce bug. And how hard it must be for children to understand when playmates and everyone else start disappearing, just as Mommy and Daddy are breaking up and hurt and angry."

"What would *you* think?"

"I think I'd wonder what was the matter with *me.*"

Abe nodded. "I might think that I was the reason for it all happening. And that's exactly what almost all children do think. That they're the cause of the split. They need to know that they're not."

"So what's your advice?"

"You ask me for advice? I don't give advice. And you should resist giving it to Karen—or her husband, if you see him. But if you just can't stop yourself, then the only kind of advice that you—or their other friends or relatives, for that matter—should give is this: Consider what's going on. Face your feelings. Deal with denials that may be unhealthy. That's the kind of advice that can be constructive—not advice about what you think people should do next."

"Abe...."

"Okay, okay. You want advice. Here's the advice of a wise and compassionate friend of mine: Stick in there. Be supportive. And listen."

We had reached the corner where I turned to go home.

"Let me know how things progress," he said. "Give me a call if you feel like it. These human puzzles are hard to put together . . . for any of us."

"I might just do that. Thanks."

"Believe me, you'd be doing me a favor. One of the hardest things for people in our profession to sort out is the uses of compassion. I'd be grateful for your insights."

Clever Abe, I thought on the way home, you knew how good that would make me feel! You also knew that *I* knew you wouldn't have said it if you hadn't meant it. Another nice little human puzzle!

# Scene Two: Early June

That conversation with Abe took place on a Tuesday, and it was ten days later, on the first Friday in June, that Jack Geary hailed me as I was entering the church. I hadn't seen Jack, literally, for years. He was a close friend of Fred's and in the old days had often been a fellow dinner guest at the Lynches'. I think Fred may have been Jack's best man when he'd married his wife, Diane. I know that the two couples bowled together, went to the movies together, and one summer went off on a camping vacation together. Come to think of it, they once even came to Sixth Church together.

Anyway, the afternoon traffic was streaming by on Forbes Avenue when a green station wagon peeled out of line and swung into the church parking lot.

"Hey, Rev!" the driver shouted. "Jack Geary. Remember me?"

"Of course, Jack," I said, laughing. "What brings you here?"

"I drive by every day on my way to and from work. I've been promising myself for some time now that I'd just look in for a minute—and today turned out to be the day." He got out of his car and we sat down together on the steps.

We caught up quickly on where the years had taken us. His wife, Diane, was keeping house and active in their eight-year-old daughter's school, seemingly content, and he was rising steadily in the retail clothing business.

He was outwardly jovial, asking me how things were in "the preacher game," but he was clearly nervous. I wondered whether it was just the usual nervousness that clergymen often evoke in people, or whether it was something more. Casting a fly over the water, I recalled what good times we'd had "back when" with the Lynches.

Jack cleared his throat. "That's ... that's one of the reasons I wanted to stop by, Will. What the hell's happened to them?"

I told him I'd been to see Karen, and that I was upset, too.

"Isn't there anything anyone can do?"

I shrugged. "I don't really know. How's Fred doing?"

"I haven't seen that much of him lately. Ran into him a week or so ago at the supermarket." He shook his head.

*  *  *

Over the years, Jack Geary had seen Fred Lynch in a lot of different situations—and confident in them all: efficient and businesslike in his patrol car; knowledgeable at ball games; precise over the backyard barbecue; and even, Jack remembered, smiling and self-assured the day he married Karen. But here was a Fred he'd never even imagined, one who looked shipwrecked halfway down aisle seven of Foodland.

"Hey, Fred! Whatcha looking for?" he called out from behind his own shopping cart.

Fred turned in both confusion and relief. "Just get me out of here, will you? I don't know what I'm looking for and I don't know where to find it!"

Jack inspected the contents of his friend's shopping cart: chocolate-covered cream-filled cupcakes, potato chips, grape soda, and a seven-dollar steak. He could imagine what Diane would say if he came home with a selection of groceries like that.

"Kids coming to you this weekend, huh?"

Fred nodded.

"Glad to see you're giving them a balanced diet."

Fred gestured in despair. "Food and kids. Nathan'll eat carrots raw but not cooked, hates peas, beans, and broccoli, will eat spinach creamed but not chopped, and told me last week that he did like cauliflower but not well enough to eat it. What's a guy to do?"

"Don't ask me, I wouldn't know," Jack answered. "Lettuce and tomatoes?"

"Good thinking. Now all we've got to do is find them."

Fred doesn't look well, Jack thought as they made their way together down the aisles. His friend's clothes were at least half a size too large. Jack wondered if he had lost a lot of weight or just looked it because of the way he was carrying himself. "How're things going in general?" he asked.

"Okay, I guess," Fred replied. "It's a rough time."

"How do things look for you and Karen?"

Fred shook his head. "It's not going to work. No way. It's better we split while we're both young enough to start again."

"You sound like your mind's made up."

"Look—who needs to be put down all the time? Living by myself in that crummy apartment is the pits, but at least I don't have to live with constant criticism. Nothing I ever cared about meant anything to Karen. Nothing I ever did was good enough. And those Sunday lunches at the country club with the Sawyers and their crowd! 'Oh, so you're Karen's husband. And what do you do?' 'I'm a policeman.' 'How nice. That must be very interesting....'" Fred shook his head. "*Nice,* for God's sake!"

"What do Nat and Sharon make of it all?"

"Who knows? I'm real confused about dealing with them. It's like we're playing a game whenever they come over. They don't say anything about the divorce, and I don't either. I don't even know whether they like coming over or not. I don't even know if I like having them come over! But when they're not there I'm lonely."

"So why haven't you given us a call when you're lonely, you old so-and-so? What are friends for?"

"Sure, sure. I know I can call you. It's just that ... well, I know Karen and Diane have been spending a lot of time together, and I guess I didn't want you guys to feel you were being dragged into the middle of something."

Jack nodded. "We can handle it. And I hope you know we'd do whatever we could to help either of you."

"Thanks," Fred said, "I know you would." He picked up a head of lettuce and dropped it into the cart. "Think one's enough?"

"Unless you've got rabbits I don't know about. Say, there's an idea—have you ever thought about pets for the kids?"

"In *my* apartment? You've got to be kidding."

At the tomato counter there were some small tomato plants on sale. "Now those, maybe, I could manage," Fred said. "The kids could watch them grow each week and then eat their own tomatoes. How about that?"

"Sure. You got a sunny place?"

"So-so. Oh heck, with my green thumb they'd probably die on me."

"What about sticking 'em in the sunny corner at the back of our yard? Then you could come over whenever you and the kids wanted to fuss around with 'em. And we could sort of keep an eye on them during the week."

Fred thought about it for a moment. "You sure? How about Diane?"

"You know it's my house, too. I'll square it with her when I get home. Leave it to me."

"Then you're on," Fred said with evident pleasure. He reached for the plants. "Four?"

"Try six. Then we'll get to enjoy the results of your labor, too."

"Thanks," Fred said as they walked to the checkout line. "That was a nice suggestion."

"No problem," Jack said. "How about having the big planting ceremony this Sunday around noon?"

"Sounds good to me."

"One other suggestion . . . ."

"What's that?"

"Bring that beautiful steak when you come. I'd hate to see it wasted on unappreciative kids."

* * *

"Come to think of it, Will, you know something?" Jack said.

"What?"

"When I first spotted Fred there in the aisle, my first thought was to get the hell out of there before he saw me."

I nodded sympathetically. "Hard to know what to say, isn't it?"

"I could feel he was really angry about everything, too. He was all choked up when he talked about his times with the children. He's really hurting. I think he ought to get out and socialize more. Stop spending so much time thinking about his problems."

"It may take some time before he feels ready for that, Jack. Maybe the best thing he can do is allow himself to feel angry and sad for a while. It's like when people need time to grieve after someone dies. They really do need that time, you know. Friends who try to cut that time short may not be doing anyone a favor."

"Yeah, but . . . I don't know."

"Maybe you'll get a better sense of what's going on when he and the kids come over this weekend. I'll bet anything he was grateful for the invitation."

"I guess so. But I'd be lying to you if I said I was looking forward to the visit. It's tough to be around people when they're like that."

"You bet it is. How does Diane feel about it all?"

Jack paused. "She and Karen are really close. But we don't talk much about it." The steeple bells chimed the hour.

He stood up. "Say, Will, it's been good to catch up with you again. That Lynch business has really been on my mind."

"And on mine, too. You know where to find me. If you come up with any bright ideas, I'd certainly like to hear them."

As he went toward his car, it occurred to me that what I'd just said had knocked the ball safely out of my court and into his. I called to him as an afterthought: "If I don't hear from you, I'll touch base in a few days to see how things are going."

He gave me a thumbs-up and a smile and then drove off.

Something kept bothering me about his visit. I was convinced that Fred and Karen's breakup was touching something deep at the Geary household. There it was—that old contagion bug. I wondered if I should have explored that with him, or at least opened a door so he could have talked about it if he'd wanted to. But after all, we'd never known each other very well. If it were he and Diane who were separating, would he have sought my help? Surely not. What did the Lynches' situation speak to in him that made him so anxious? Did it echo some of his own marital problems, known or unknown but dimly felt? I suppose I could have asked Jack some of these questions if I'd thought about them at the time. Then again, it would have been pretty presumptuous of me to turn the conversation around to his personal life.

# SCENE THREE: MID-JUNE

As if to make up for the late spring, summer came early. Overnight everyone was complaining of the heat instead of the cold. The third Monday in June, a day off for me, was still, hot, and cloudless—a real beauty. I felt incredibly alive and, after a couple of leisurely mugs of coffee and the morning paper, I packed my dog, Cindy, into my Jeep and headed for the countryside. We whiled away most of the morning following our noses in whatever directions seemed alluring, and along about noon I decided it was time to get something to eat. I reckoned that I couldn't be too far from Saxonburg and its well-known country inn. I took a look at the map and saw that a slight detour would bring me out near where Fred's parents, Dwight and Ruth Lynch, lived. Why not? I thought. I'd often dropped in on them before on my days off, and they'd always been warm and welcoming.

I found their driveway without difficulty—a lane that led up a gentle rise to the hillock where the Lynches, both now well into their sixties, watched over the growth and harvest of their farm life. I parked my Jeep beside the barn and walked nearly a full circle around it before I found Dwight inside, tinkering with an old pickup.

"It *is* you, Will!" Dwight exclaimed, wiping his hands and shaking mine firmly. "Thought I recognized the sound of that motor. Have you eaten?"

"Something cold to drink would be good, Dwight," I said. "I was planning to stop in Saxonburg on the way home."

"Hell," he said, "why go spending the church's money when you can eat for free? And let that poor dog out of your wagon. Can't get into any trouble around here."

So that's the way the morning ended up—around a bowl of freshly-made chicken salad and muffins, with Ruth insisting I must still be hungry long after I felt full to the brim. Dwight looked just grand, I thought, but Ruth had a weariness about her which I attributed to age and, perhaps, to being a good deal overweight. Dwight, as it turned out, was quite concerned about his wife's health, and as we walked down after lunch to inspect a new irrigation project he was working on, he made no bones about it.

"That woman better lose some of that weight or she's not going to be around to keep me in order much longer," he said. "The doctor's real worried about her blood pressure. She knows it, too, but can't seem to do much about it."

I suggested that Fred's and Karen's separation was probably proving very hard for them both.

"It is hard for us, Will," he admitted, sitting on a stump by the stream. "It's a big disappointment. Mind you, I always told Fred he should have finished college, and if he had, I bet things would have turned out different. Not much you can do nowadays without that piece of paper, though it sometimes seems that there isn't a whole hell of a lot a man can find to do *with* it, either. All the same, he sure narrowed his chances."

As we talked, I came to understand that Dwight was feeling deeply hurt over something else. Fred had never told his father that he and Karen were in trouble; he'd simply broken the news of the separation the day after he moved out.

"Ruth and I just feel kind of left out. If we'd known Fred was having problems all this time, we'd sure have wanted to help. Can't say I know what we might have done, but that's a hard thing to go through for anyone. And those poor kids in the middle of it all! I guess that's what we worry about most right now."

"I've found that people often leave their parents out of their troubles for a long time," I said. "Somehow telling your folks about problems at home makes them more real. Maybe more real than we're ready to admit."

"Could be," he said with a shrug.

"But we all need to feel needed at times like that, don't we? Particularly by the ones we love."

"That's for sure," he said. "At least I know those little kids need us. Why, only two weeks ago Fred dropped them off here for the day, and Nat and I got into some talk that's made me wonder a good deal ever since. It was a tad on the cool side for ice cream that day, but ice cream was what he wanted to make."

\* \* \*

"Looks like it's getting hard to turn," Dwight Lynch said.

Nathan nodded. "Sure is, Gramps."

"That's good."

"Good? My arm's killing me!" Nathan let go of the ice cream freezer's crank. "What's good about it?"

"Because that means it's almost done. Here, let me spell you. You can take over the ice chopping."

"We're going to need *more*?"

"Little more ice, little more salt...Give me a hand draining this thing."

Dwight pulled the plug and together they tilted the freezer. As the water poured out, Nathan asked, "How long 'til we can eat it?"

His grandfather smiled. "Well, let's see now. A while to finish up...a while for it to set...a while for us to do some errands...a while for lunch...."

"Oh, Gramps!" Nathan protested.

"Why, Nat, you're not in a hurry or anything, are you?"

"Gramps, stop teasing. How long, really?"

"Nana will scoop it out for us right after lunch. Okay?"

"I guess so," Nathan said.

"Come on, get going. Ice...salt...."

They worked in silence for a few moments.

This grandson of mine is really sprouting, Dwight thought. A few months ago, I don't think he'd have been able to turn the crank at all. Sharon's a cute little tyke, too. Stubborn, though.

"I like coming over here, Gramps," Nathan said.

"Glad to hear it," his grandfather replied. "Nana and I sure like having you." He noticed his grandson scowling as he hacked away at the ice. "How are things at home?"

Nathan shrugged.

"Both good and bad, I guess, huh?" his grandfather said.

"I can't seem to do anything right when I'm with Mom. She's always telling me to do this or do that, and I try, but she always finds something wrong with it."

"She's got a lot more to do now that your dad isn't living there. I guess she counts on you for all kinds of things you didn't have to do before."

Nathan packed some more ice around the churn and sprinkled on some salt.

"Gramps. . . ."

"Yes?"

"Why did Dad go away?"

Dwight pulled an old bandanna out of his hip pocket and wiped his forehead. "You know something, Nat? Nana and I have wondered the same thing. A lot. Why do *you* think your dad left?"

The boy jabbed at the earth with his ice pick. "Because he didn't love us anymore, I guess." His tears spilled over in spite of his effort to blink them away.

Kids' logic sure is hard to work with, Dwight thought, moving over to his grandson and taking him in his arms. I guess there are some things they just can't understand . . . especially about grown-ups. "He loves you very, very much, Nat. He's very sad not to be living with you and Sharon. Come on now, dry those tears. Everything's going to be okay."

"He didn't have to go if he didn't want to."

"Hey, just a minute now, Nat," Dwight said. "You've got no cause to get sore at your dad. He felt he had to move away from your mother because they were making each other very unhappy. He didn't want to move away from *you*. I love your dad because he's my son. His leaving doesn't make any difference to the way I love him. And he loves you because you're *his* son. His moving away from your mother doesn't make any difference to the way he loves you, either. Can you understand that a little?"

Nathan nodded.

"Then let's wrap this old blanket around the churn to keep the cold in and we'll get going. The sooner we get our errands done, the sooner we'll be home."

"And the sooner we're home, the sooner I'll get to lick the dasher," said Nathan with a little smile.

Dwight felt relieved to be back on safe ground. Their moods sure change fast at that age, he reflected. Like March weather . . . and just as well.

"Climb into the car and we'll head for the shopping center," Dwight told his grandson. "Nana needs a few things, and you can help me pick them out."

Nathan was his usual self as they rambled from store to store. On the way back, he grew quiet again. Then Dwight heard him take a deep breath.

"Gramps. . . ."

"Yes, Nat?"

"Gramps, do you think I could come live with you?"

Hoo, boy, Dwight thought. How'm I supposed to handle this one? "Why do you think you'd like to do that?" he asked.

"I just like being with you and Nana. I'd be happier here."

"Well, Nat, I'll tell you something," he said carefully, keeping his eyes on the road ahead. "I think the best place for children to grow up is with their parents. Sure, there are hassles, but that's part of growing up too. You know one reason why we have such a good time together?"

"Why?"

"Nana and I don't have to tell you to pick up your room, brush your teeth, do your homework, turn off the TV, go to bed, and all that sort of stuff. That's for parents to do, just like Nana and I did it with your father and Aunt Gloria when they were growing up. To tell you the truth, I kind of like being a grandfather right now. And to be a grandfather, I need a grandson, don't I?"

"I guess so," Nathan said. They were pulling into the driveway.

"But I'll make you a promise, Nat."

The boy looked at him expectantly.

"If ever there was a time when your mother and father thought they couldn't take care of you properly, you could always move right in here with us. Lickety-split. Is that a deal?"

Nathan nodded. As they drew up beside the house he exclaimed, "Gramps! The ice cream's gone!"

"Guess Nana's taken it into the kitchen. You'd better hop in there and stop her from licking that dasher herself."

"She wouldn't. Not without me!"

"You never know. If I were you, I'd get in there quick."

Nat hopped out of the car, leaving the door open, and shouted, "Nana, I'm back! Wait for me! Wait for me!"

*   *   *

"I love having that boy around, Will," Dwight said, "but I'll tell you something. I wouldn't want to be a parent again. Not for all the tea in China!" He flung a pebble into the stream.

"Again? Don't you still think of yourself as a parent, for heaven's sake?"

My tone must have been more aggressive than I'd intended, for he looked taken aback.

"Fred's different," he said curtly. "He's all grown up and on his own."

"He's still your son," I insisted. "You can't just resign as his father."

We stood up and walked on a way in silence.

"Do you see him much?"

"Oh, he's out here all the time," Dwight said. "Mopes around, mostly."

"You sound mad at him. Why?"

He sat down on a log and mopped the top of his head. "Cause we're all in this confounded mess," he said. "I did the best I knew how by that boy the whole time he was growing up, and I guess it just wasn't good enough."

I know it must have hurt him to say that. "These things are hard on everyone, aren't they?"

"Uh-huh," he said, "it's a tough one. We've come to love Karen like one of our own. She's a good girl. Why, she and Ruth were on the phone together the other night, and both ended up in tears before they were through."

"I'm glad Karen knows you love her. I know she's always felt very close to you both. I wouldn't be surprised if her folks felt the same way you do—I mean, that they're somehow to blame for a marriage that didn't work. But, like you say, she's a good girl. I don't think it's the Sawyers' fault, do you?"

Dwight shook his head. "No, they're well-meaning people. Just as heartsick about it all as we are. We drove to town and had lunch with them a couple of weeks ago. Ruth thought we should all get together after this ruckus started, so she just called them right up and they took us to lunch out at their country club. What we talked about didn't add up to a hill of beans, but it was cordial enough."

"When you're hurt, it's easy to feel angry. And that you're to blame. It sounds like Nat may have been feeling some of those things, too. He sure is lucky to have you to talk to. And to cry with."

"I hate to see him cry, Will. Or get mad at his dad like that. He's got no cause to."

"I wonder," I said. "If I were Nat, I might think that it was something bad I'd done that made my mom and dad split up, and I'm sure I'd be mad as the dickens at my dad for going off and leaving me. That's a lot to feel sad and angry about. Sure, I might be wrong about it all, but there's no way I could know that unless someone let me feel those feelings and helped me understand what was really going on. If I were little, I'd want that someone to be a person I loved and who loved me back. Like a grandfather I knew I could trust."

There was a long silence then. Downstream, the undergrowth crackled and parted and out bounded Cindy—panting, wet, and obviously pleased with herself.

"Sure is a pretty dog!" said Dwight. Cindy shook herself all over us and then rolled in the dirt at our feet.

"Was," I laughed. "Now you know why I travel around in that old Jeep."

As we headed back toward the house, Dwight asked, "Your folks still alive, Will?"

"Mom died about four years ago. Dad's doing fine. He lives in a retirement community in North Carolina. It turned out to be a great place for him. He's real happy."

"Are the two of you close?"

"We are, even though we don't have many daily things in common. He spends a lot of his time in madras pants on the golf course, and I spend a lot of my time in a dark suit in church. I'm going to try it his way for a few days when I go on vacation the beginning of July, and I'm looking forward to it. We have a good time when we're together. We don't talk a lot about our lives, but we take real pleasure in each other's company. I think it's because we know that whatever we do and wherever we are, there'll never be a relationship for us quite like the one we have together. Sometimes I'm afraid we're even a little smug about it."

"I like that," Dwight said. "Something tells me he was a good dad to you."

"*Is* a good dad, Dwight," I corrected him.

# Scene Four: Late June

Tidying up loose ends in preparation for my July getaway kept me plenty busy after my afternoon with the Lynches. One of the loose ends was my getting back to Jack Geary, which I had promised to do but had let slide. I dialed his number early one evening, got Diane, and she called Jack in from the back yard, where he was getting the barbecue fired up for supper. I apologized for dragging him to the phone and explained that I just wanted to touch base before leaving town.

"And how did the great tomato-planting party with Fred and the kids go?" I asked.

"It didn't," he replied. "Nope, I'm afraid that didn't work out. Look, could I stop by and see you after work tomorrow? I'm just getting the coals started, and . . . ."

"That'd be fine. I'll be waiting for you in my office."

"Great. See you then."

Jack bounded in shortly after 5:30 the following day. That was when I learned what had happened to the plans he'd made with Fred when they'd met in the grocery store.

"You might say Diane and I had a little disagreement," he began.

*   *   *

Jack was in the kitchen putting away the groceries when Diane came up the back stairs with a basket of clean laundry.

"Get everything?" she asked.

"Except the chicken breasts. They were out."

Diane emptied the basket onto the kitchen table and started sorting through the pile. "Oh well, hamburgers again. . . ."

"I saw Fred at the store," Jack said.

"Did you talk to him?"

"Of course."

"I wouldn't have."

"Oh Diane, for heaven's sake. . . . In fact, I invited him and the kids over on Sunday to start a tomato patch in a corner of our garden."

Diane stared at her husband in disbelief. "You did *what?*" she exclaimed, her voice rising.

"We were talking about his weekends with the kids, and I thought it might be nice for them to have a reason to get out of Fred's apartment and do something together."

"Well, that's mighty big of you!" She turned on him, hands braced on the counter behind her. "Don't you think you could have asked me first to see how *I* felt about it?"

"I didn't think I had to. Friends are friends, after all."

"After what he's done to *my* best friend, it really didn't occur to you that I might not want him hanging around here?"

"Hey, cool down. Think what it could mean for Nathan and Sharon. You're not being reasonable at all."

"What's 'reasonable' in all this? Fred's walking out on Karen? I'm all in favor of helping the kids any way we can, but Fred Lynch isn't planting any tomatoes in my garden."

"*Our* garden."

Diane went back to folding clothes. "I don't understand you. I really don't."

"The feeling's mutual," Jack muttered, stuffing the last grocery bag into the drawer and walking out of the kitchen. In the living room, Jennifer, their eight-year-old daughter, was watching television. "Turn that thing off," he said, dropping into an armchair and picking up the newspaper.

The game-show chatter ceased. "Will you play catch with me?" Jennifer asked.

"I . . . ." Jack started to say that he wanted to read the paper but changed his mind. "Sure, Jeffie. Let's do that."

"Why were you and Mom shouting?" Jennifer asked as they were throwing the ball back and forth.

"It was nothing," Jack answered. "We . . . we were just having a difference of opinion about something. Why?"

"I just wondered, that's all."

Jack threw his daughter a grounder. Jennifer reached for it but the ball skipped past her. "I can't *ever* get those," she complained.

"Get right behind it. Keep your glove out in front of you." Jack sent her another. The ball took an unexpected bounce, Jennifer shied away, and the ball rolled down to the end of the garden. She hurled her glove after it.

"Don't get discouraged," Jack called. "You'll start picking 'em up soon, you'll see."

They worked on grounders and flies for a while until Jennifer called a halt for a drink. As they were sitting on the back steps, she said, "Dad, last time Sharon Lynch was over visiting she said she didn't have a father anymore. What happened to him?"

"Nothing happened to him," Jack said, irritated that the subject of the Lynch family situation had come up again. "Mr. and Mrs. Lynch have separated. They may get divorced. Anyway, he isn't living with them anymore."

"But he's still Sharon's father, isn't he?"

"Of course he is. Sharon and Nathan go visit him on weekends. More lemonade?"

Jennifer shook her head. "No, thanks." After a pause, she said, "Could you and Mom ever get a divorce?"

Jack felt his exasperation mounting. "Look," he said, "lots of people we know have gotten divorces. If a husband and wife are very unhappy living together and can't work out their problems, that's what sometimes happens. Your mom and I don't have any plans to get a divorce."

"But sometimes you don't get along. . . ."

"No two people get along *all* the time," Jack said. "We've always worked out our differences so far, and that's what we'll go on doing. Don't worry about it, okay?"

"Okay," his daughter said. "I guess."

Later that evening, finally settling down to read the paper while Diane sewed a patch on a pair of Jennifer's jeans, Jack was still distracted by the irritations of the afternoon. There was also the lingering issue of the tomato patch. He knew that the issue was decided; it just had to be resolved. Diane was wrong, he continued to feel. Then again, who needed all the emotional wear-and-tear this business was bringing into their family? Tomato patch or no tomato patch, there would still be Karen's frequent visits, sometimes with the children, and now he wondered how healthy it was for Jeffie to be subjected to other people's confused children.

"So what do I tell Fred?" he asked, putting the paper aside.

Diane looked up from her work. "Why don't you tell him the truth? Tell him I can't deal with being pulled between the two of them, that I feel a special loyalty to Karen, and that I'd find it too difficult to have him coming around all the time."

"That's easy to say."

"Do you want me to call him? It wouldn't bother me at all."

He felt stung by some implicit slur on his courage. "No," he said, "I'll do it."

She came around behind his chair and put her arms around his neck. "I'm sorry, honey," she said. "Maybe I'm overreacting. But why do we have to make all their problems our problems?"

"I told you I'd call him," he replied.

She sighed and went to put her sewing things away. Folding the pair of jeans, she asked, "Coming upstairs?"

He shook his head and reached for the paper. "I'll be up in a while," he said.

\* \* \*

"So I got hold of Fred the next day and called it all off. It didn't seem there was much else I could do," Jack explained.

"What did he say?" I asked.

"He said he wasn't surprised. He said he'd figured Diane would have trouble dividing her loyalties like that. Let's see.... He sounded kind of sad and resigned, said he was glad Karen had a good friend, and said he'd plant the damn things in his own back yard. I was still all roiled up about it and mad as hell at Diane. He told me to forget it."

"And did you?"

"Me? No way! I stew about things like that. Diane's always been much more straight from the shoulder. You know what she's thinking as soon as she thinks it. I was ticked off at her for a week. I still feel bad about it."

"I'm sorry, Jack," I said. "That was a nice idea you had, and I can imagine how you felt about having to give it up. Loyalties can be hard to handle at times like this. Have you and Diane gotten over it?"

"Oh, sure. We get in and out of these hot spots all the time. They don't really mean anything."

"That's good," I said. "My folks had their go-arounds, too. I remember one summer—I must have been around Jennifer's age—I was sure they were going to get a divorce. It scared me to death. It took me quite a while to realize that blowups can blow over, and that it's okay for people who love each other to get really mad at each other. That's not an easy thing for a kid to understand."

"Hell, Will, Jeffie'd never think that her mom and me would split up just because we got mad once in a while."

"Maybe not. But right now she's watching Fred and Karen deal with their anger in exactly that way. She knows it *can* happen."

"Now you've got me worried."

"Didn't mean to. Just a thought."

"Yeah . . . well . . . . Hey, Rev, I'm glad we had this chance to talk. Airing it kind of helps it all blow over."

"Just don't forget Jennifer, that's all. She may be watching you and Diane pretty closely for a while."

Jack nodded. "I'll mention it to Diane, too. You have a good vacation, okay?"

"I plan to, Jack."

I succeeded, what's more, spending a week with my dad in North Carolina and then three more visiting friends on an island off the Maine coast. I managed to leave most of my daily concerns back in Pittsburgh, where they belonged, but I did take with me the puzzle of the relationship among love, loyalty, and anger. I chewed it over a good deal as I traveled, and I decided that one day I'd try to address that relationship in public.

# Scene Five: August

And so I did, preaching a sermon about it the last Sunday in August. I wasn't entirely satisfied with the results, but at least I'd taken one step forward in my thinking by treating both anger and loyalty as aspects of something else—compassion.

The text I used was Ephesians 4:15: "Speak the truth in the spirit of love." What I tried to convey was that being loyal to a friend "through thick and thin" doesn't necessarily mean defending that friend unquestioningly. It's possible to be loyal by continuing to *accept* that friend whether or not you think his or her actions are defensible. There's nothing about loyalty that says you have to be blind or uncritical. Loyalty leaves plenty of room to say to a friend, "Hey, wait a minute! You're way out of line!" And suppose that provokes anger? No matter. There's nothing wrong with anger that's based on caring and understanding—on *compassion.*

How the sermon went over I don't know. Like always, everyone said either "That was a lovely sermon" or said nothing. But I felt good about it anyway.

Far down the line of exiting parishioners, I saw someone who looked like Karen but with white hair. I kept glancing in her direction, but she kept dropping back in the line until she was at its end. I shook hand after hand, exchanging pleasantries, until at last she and I were face to face.

"Reverend Morgan," she said, smiling shyly. "How is my little neighbor boy?"

It was Virginia Sawyer, Karen's mother, and I gave her a hug. I don't think I'd seen her since Dad retired.

"You look wonderful," I said.

"I do?" she said, her voice lilting into a question. "I looked better a few months ago. I can't go to your father's pharmacy anymore, so I decided to try to find my cure here." Her tone was light, but that was only a prelude to the tearful seriousness that came as we sat together in the stillness of the empty church.

"I'd do anything to save Karen's marriage," she said. "But I can't, and it breaks my heart."

She went on to tell me about her last encounter with Fred—last in the sense of most recent and probably final.

\* \* \*

"It's been a long time since you made me a cake like that," Bill Sawyer said, watching his wife spread the dark chocolate icing over the even darker cake underneath. "What have I done to merit such a reward?"

Virginia smiled at him. "Just been your usual wonderful self," she said.

"How nice to know I'm appreciated," he said, putting his arms around her. "For Karen and the kids?"

She shook her head. "You're close. It's for Fred and the kids. They'll be with him for the weekend."

"You're still hoping to get them back together, aren't you?"

She nodded and went on with the finishing touches.

"You're amazing," he said. "Personally, I think it's the best thing that could happen to Karen. Fred's okay, but I never did think he was right for her. Not ambitious enough. He's soft. He could have been making $35,000 a year if he'd come to work for me. Maybe he'd even be running the place. Now that I've retired, there's not much I can do for him. So the cake is meant to sweeten the conversation, is it?"

She wiped her hands on her apron. "You could put it that way. . . ."

"Scheming woman," he said, shaking his head. "You never did know when to give up."

She looked pleased with herself. Putting a large plastic cover over the cake, she picked it up carefully and headed for the door. He opened it for her.

"Good luck," he said.

"Keys in the car?" she asked.

He nodded.

"Okay," she said. "See you later."

As she eased the Seville out of the garage, the cake secured by the safety belt on the seat beside her, she was already planning her approach. Would Fred think she was interfering? Not if she didn't seem to be telling him what to do. Would he be hostile or angry toward her? Probably not, as long as she wasn't openly critical. *Reasonableness,* that was the key, she had decided by the time she arrived at Fred's apartment. And if he were reasonable, he couldn't help seeing how little he had to lose—and how much everyone had to gain—by staying married to Karen.

But after a short period of forced small talk, it no longer seemed quite so simple.

"I can't explain it," Fred said. They had each eaten a piece of the cake, and he was standing by the window looking out into the noisy street. Virginia Sawyer sat on the sofa stirring a mug of coffee. "We're just going in two different directions, and we've got to get out of each other's way."

"But I don't see any reason why both of you can't get what you want out of life and stay together."

"She finds being married to a policeman bad enough without being married to a carpenter and living in the middle of nowhere. But that's where I'm going. Another ten years and I'll have my pension. I won't even be forty-five. And after that I'm going to settle down in some small town in the hills and open a cabinet-making business. You know what Karen says about all that?"

Virginia ignored the question. "You'll need money to do that, Fred."

"I'll have it."

"Not much."

"Enough."

"Bill and I won't live forever, you know. In ten years we'll either be old or gone. Bill's done well, and Karen will have a tidy little inheritance one day. That could help you."

"But it couldn't help *us*. I couldn't stand living off of Karen's money, I'll tell you that right now."

What an exasperating man, Virginia thought . . . so self-centered. "What about the children?" she said. "Don't you think you ought to consider them? We know what happens to children from broken homes."

"I am thinking about the kids. What happens to kids who grow up in so-called 'happy' homes? Are they any better off? I've seen enough kids in trouble on the streets— the good streets as well as the lousy ones. One day I'm going to have a place for mine where there's air and space and . . . ."

Virginia waved a hand impatiently. "For heaven's sake, they'll be grown up by then. In the meantime, I'd be less than honest if I didn't tell you that I think you're being very selfish by insisting on having everything your own way. All Karen wants is a civilized life." She looked around the tiny apartment, noting the second-hand furniture and the flaking paint around the hot-water pipes. "You have to admit, this isn't much of a place for children, even on weekends."

"We manage okay, thanks," he said shortly. "Anyway, I think I'll be moving soon."

"Oh?"

"I've applied to the State Police Academy in Hershey."

"Then you'll be leaving town. Speaking frankly, I think that will be better for everyone."

"I'll still see the kids on weekends. It's not that far."

She rose to go. "I really don't have anything else to say, Fred. You used to be such a reasonable man. I don't understand what's gotten into you. But whatever it is you want, I think you're making a big mistake going about it this way."

"I guess we all change," he said, seeing her to the door. She offered her hand.

"Thank you for the cake," he said.

"Goodbye," she said.

On the way home, Virginia reflected that now she had done all she could do. If he goes through with it, she thought, Karen and the children will need all the support they can get. We can't let his bizarre notions wreck their lives.

*   *   *

"And I won't let him wreck their lives," Virginia insisted. "We'll just have to find a way to do without him."

I nodded. Talk about ambivalence ... and I mean my own! I was literally without words because of the surge of anger I felt. Had she heard *nothing* of my sermon on compassion? But I was angriest at my own anger. Where was *my* compassion? I was so unsure of what I was going to do with my feelings at that moment that I got up and walked halfway down the aisle and back again. It crossed my mind that it would have served Virginia right if I had kept on walking up to the empty pulpit and shouted my sermon all over again, right at her.

"Well," she said, "I'm sure you've got other things to do...."

"No," I said sharply, turning back to her, "I've got nothing more important to do right now than to tell you what I'm feeling." She showed clear surprise at the edge I couldn't keep out of my voice. "Look," I went on, "I can understand why you feel the way you do. You're hurt. You're disappointed. You're angry. Maybe somewhere deep inside, you wonder whether you had something to do with what's gone wrong—either as a parent or as an in-law.

"Fine! We're all going to feel those feelings when something like this happens. So go ahead and feel them, but for God's sake keep them in their place! Righteous indignation isn't going to do anything for Nat and Sharon.

Starting a spite war isn't, either. The worst thing you can do for them is to start driving an emotional wedge between them and their father."

If she was surprised before, she was quite visibly shaken now—and so, I confess, was I. But I was beginning to feel better, too.

"I simply said I would not let him wreck their lives," she said.

"And that you all would just find a way to do without him," I reminded her. "That's one thing those children should *not* be made to do. No matter how you feel about Fred, or Karen feels about Fred, or you feel about what Fred has done to Karen, there is one truth that you are all going to have to keep in mind: that Nat and Sharon *need their father.* They need him now, and they're going to go on needing him as they grow. Allowing Fred to be their father is not going to wreck their lives. In fact, depriving them of their father, or making them feel they have a 'bad' father, is much more likely to have sad consequences for them."

Virginia took a handkerchief from her pocketbook and dabbed her eyes. "Oh, Will," she sighed, "why couldn't they simply have stayed together? Then we wouldn't have had to worry about the children. Nobody has a totally happy marriage, after all."

My sudden anger was gone and I once again felt compassion for this woman—compassion for anyone caught like this in such a hurtful, human predicament.

Sitting down beside her again, I said, "Virginia, there's one thing I feel very sure of. Children can come through almost anything if they feel loved and protected by the important adults in their lives. Those adults don't have to love each other. Please try not to let grown-up problems destroy what Nat and Sharon need to feel from everyone in their family—parents and grandparents alike. Think about that."

"I'll be very honest with you, Will," she said. "I know what you're saying to me is true. But I don't know if I can

-46-

do it. Or even, really, how to do it. But yes, I will think about it."

I walked her to the door of the church. "It's hard for any of us to practice what we preach," I said. She smiled at that as she left.

There was something I found myself wondering about later that afternoon: the whole question of "staying together for the sake of the children." Was it a valid consideration? Like so many questions, the answer, I felt sure, was sometimes yes and sometimes no. What made the difference? On an impulse, I picked up the phone and called Abe Lewi at home. I didn't even apologize for bothering him on a weekend, but from his tone you'd have thought our previous conversation had never ended.

"What makes the difference?" he replied to my question. "Okay, here's what I think. When there continue to be avenues of communication and affection open between the husband and wife, the children might be a reason for really trying to resolve the conflict before settling for a separation. But when both parties want out, staying together for the children's sake may not be helpful for them."

"Because of the inevitable tensions they'll feel?" I asked.

"Sure. But from our perspective, it's more than that. Let's take your particular example. Sharon is . . . how old?"

"She's five."

"Like most girls that age, she's probably identifying closely with her mother. She may even be adopting some of her mother's mannerisms. This is happening at a time when the father is angry about lots of things that the mother does. Or take a boy of Nathan's age—he's seven, right?"

"He just turned eight."

"Then he's at the point when he may be incorporating aspects of his father that send his mother into a rage. You can see how a child's healthy affiliation with a parent of the same sex could get very complicated in this type of situation."

"So it might be best for the parents to split up," I mused.

"All I'd say is this: I don't know of anything in the research literature that proves that children from divorced families have a higher risk of emotional problems than do children from families where both parents are present. In other words, having parents who are married or divorced does not in itself determine the emotional well-being of the child. For instance, the quality of the relationships that a child has with other adults in his or her environment can really shape and interpret for a child just what a divorce means. Or a marriage, for that matter."

"You mean relatives and friends. . . ."

"'Important others,' as we like to call them. They're crucial in any child's healthy emotional development. And they're crucial for us adults, too."

We talked for a few minutes more. Abe, as usual, had given me a lot to think about.

I dimly remembered the phrase "important others" from a college psychology course, but it hadn't surfaced in my mind for years. As I recalled, an "important other" was someone other than the primary caregivers—the mother and father—who was both close and yet somewhat distanced; someone who, through mutual trust, was able to help a child confirm his or her sense of self-worth.

Who had been the "important others" in my own life? It took me only a moment to sort through the cast of adult characters who had peopled my childhood and pick out my godfather, Jerry Flack. Jerry and my dad had gone to college together, and they stayed close friends the rest of their lives. When I first knew him, Jerry was flying for a regional airline, but he soon joined Pan American and went on to captain some of their international flights. I can remember to this day how angry I was when he and his family moved to Los Angeles. I felt betrayed and abandoned. I couldn't imagine why he would go and do that to me. Ah, what self-centered worlds we inhabit as children! We really do feel that we're the belly button of the universe. The first time Jerry came back to visit, I didn't talk to him for a full three minutes.

His world seemed heroic—his uniform, his flights, his tales about distant cities. What sticks in my mind most clearly is a picture of him in old-fashioned dungarees and a plaid shirt, fussing with pieces of machinery in his basement. I spent hours with him down there. Although my little life at home and school seemed dull to me, Jerry had a way, as I talked about what I was doing, of making my world and my problems seem important—and me important within it all. I'd go home feeling that I *could* be whatever I wanted to be when I grew up.

If my family had gone through a divorce—which, thank heavens, it never did—I'd have wanted Jerry around. He'd have managed to let me know that even though my world was coming apart, it wasn't coming to an end.

Who, I wondered, were Nat's and Sharon's "important others"? Their grandparents, to be sure. But the Lynches weren't easily accessible to the children; as for the Sawyers, I felt that the whole business of taking sides might not be making them as supportive as they might be.

Karen was an only child, so the children would have no uncles and aunts on that side. And Fred.... Of course! There was his sister, Gloria. I'd lost track of her since she married, but I remembered her well from the old days. From the little I knew about astrology, I'd say she was a true Leo if ever there was one! If she hadn't moved out of town, it would be interesting to get together. Maybe she could shed a new light on the situation.

I jotted a note to myself to find out if she was in fact still around. Then, out of curiosity, I jotted down the names of all the people I had happened to talk to so far: Karen, Jack Geary, Dwight Lynch, Virginia Sawyer . . . and it struck me forcefully that missing from the list was Fred himself. That omission, in turn, made me think about where I was going with these people.

When I'd met with Karen, I'd felt hopelessly inadequate. But it was from her that I began to learn something important: While I couldn't really *do* anything for her or the children, I could, instead, try to *be* something to them.

Most people want help in finding their own answers. One person's solution won't necessarily work for another; that's how unique each of us is in this world. Abe Lewi had talked to me about the limits caregivers find placed on their caregiving abilities. The more I was coming to accept those limitations, the more comfortable and confident I felt.

I wasn't sure what use I'd been to Jack Geary, but perhaps our talks and my listening had helped him to sort out some things—his own feelings, what he thought Fred was going through, and his daughter Jennifer's reactions. The same could probably be said for the time I'd spent with Dwight Lynch. Maybe that had started him thinking about his own feelings of anger and denial and Nat's feelings of anger and possible guilt. Once again, though, I had to accept that Jack's and Dwight's next move was up to them.

My own initial feelings of anger toward Virginia worried me a little, but I decided to view them as a sign of my growing confidence and ability to speak out. I'd been aggressive, that's true, but I don't think I'd been hostile. She'd certainly made me see how a relative's reactions to a husband-wife breakup could easily and inadvertently lead to the weakening of other important relationships, such as that between parent and child. I hoped that my strong response had brought that insight into focus for her, too.

If I was trying to *be* something rather than *do* something, what was I trying to be? I concluded that I was trying, in my own limited way, to be a kind of "important other"—present, available, concerned, and certainly caring. For I did care about them all. It was time to let Fred know it, too—in person.

# Scene Six: Early September

So I called Fred, told him that I knew he was going through a rough period, and said I'd like to see him.

"Hey, that's really nice of you to call, Will," he said, "but everything's okay. I mean, we all seem to be getting through it and . . . ."

Quietly, I interrupted him. "Fred, I want to see you as an old friend."

He hesitated, and then he asked, "Whatcha doing Thursday evening?"

We met at a pizza parlor around the corner from where he lived. I had hoped to get a look at his apartment and to have a quiet place where we could talk, but, clearly, that wasn't what Fred had in mind. So we talked as best we could over the jangle and confusion of the pinball machines and a busy take-out crowd. The conversation wasn't easy, and I found myself telling him a lot about my daily life and opening up more than I'd meant to about the frustrations of the profession I'd chosen.

"I guess we all have them," he said, and went on to share with me some of what he wryly referred to as "the joys of being a Law Enforcement Officer." After hearing what he told me, I wasn't surprised that he was hoping his application to the State Police Academy would be accepted.

"How are Nat and Sharon doing?" I asked.

He shrugged. "I really don't know. I mean, how do you tell?"

"But you see them often?"

"Every other weekend for sure, and sometimes in between."

"Do you have a good time together?"

"Oh, pretty much. It's just that . . . I guess I need to see them more than they need to see me. And lots of times we seem to run out of things to do. It's hard sometimes. Like the last weekend we spent together. . . ."

*   *   *

Fred saw the double jump but didn't take it. Instead, he moved a man ahead from his king's row. "Okay, hon, your move. Think hard."

Sharon, lying on her stomach, her chin in one hand, surveyed the board. She moved a piece ahead into danger, kept her finger on it, and moved it back. "Hey," she said. "I get to huff you! See? You could of jumped."

"Okay for you, Sharp Eyes. You're learning too fast. Hmmmmm. What shall I do now?"

Outside the open back door, a garbage can clattered. There was a moment of silence and then a howl of pain. Fred jumped to his feet and ran toward the door. "You okay, Nat?" he shouted.

Nat, still straddling his downed bike, lay on the cobblestones grimacing through his tears. He shook his head. "My knee . . . ," he managed to say.

Fred carefully disentangled his son from the bike frame and carried him into the house. His left knee was scraped and bleeding.

"Boy, I'll bet that hurts," Fred said, "but it doesn't look serious." He hugged Nat close. "Let's go into the bathroom and fix it up."

The boy winced as his father swabbed the wound with water. "I know," Fred said. "Just a tad more and we'll be done." He gently patted the raw spots dry and reached for the can of disinfectant.

"This won't sting," he said. "It'll just feel cold." All the same, he felt Nat's hand grip his shoulder.

A few moments later, the injury was neatly bound with gauze and adhesive tape. "Hey," Fred said, giving his son a kiss, "I'm proud of you. I really am."

"Can I still go swimming, Dad?"

Fred shook his head. "'Fraid not. They won't let you in the pool like that."

"But I want to go!" Sharon chimed in. "You said I could!"

"Sure, hon, we'll still go. We'll get you something to read on the way, Nat, okay? We won't stay at the pool for long."

As they walked to the Y with Nat holding his hand and Sharon skipping on ahead, Fred thought about how much he loved these children. It was a painful love now that he saw them only on the weekends, and he knew that their visits would be even less frequent if the job came through at the Police Academy. But it wasn't just the times of separation that were hard. The times together were, too. How could he ever tell them how he felt—about them, or about his bitterness toward their mother? He had resigned himself to believing that their feelings would always be a mystery to him.

How different our reality is from the way it must look right now, Fred mused as they strolled past a row of houses. Anyone looking out one of those windows would assume that I'm a happy father out for a stroll with his happy kids on a warm afternoon. How different our three realities are—mine, and Nat's, and Sharon's. With no way to bridge the gap.

The pool at the Y was crowded, but there was room in the shallow end for him to help Sharon practice her dog paddle. He supported her little round belly with the palm of his hand as she splashed and struggled to reach the edge of the pool, turning then to fling her arms around his neck and wind her legs around his waist.

"Was I swimming, Daddy?" she asked breathlessly. "Was I?"

"Almost," he said. "You're getting there."

Her body was cold and slippery against his, and in her delighted laughter he suddenly heard the laugh of a much older girl, going out with boys, facing the uncertainties of adolescence and then marriage. . . . Would he be around then when she might need him? Or would he have become a distant stranger she hardly knew? Would she have a new "daddy" she loved more than she loved him?

"How about it, hon? Had enough? I don't want you getting cold."

"Just one more time, okay?" she begged. "Please?"

"Okay," he said. "Just one."

Later they sat together around the kitchen table for supper. A lighted candle flickered on the blue-and-white tablecloth.

"Yuk," said Nat. "Broccoli. Mom never gives us broccoli."

"I wish you wouldn't complain about everything I try to feed you, Nat," Fred said. "It's getting to be a drag, you know that?"

"I don't complain about everything," Nat replied, poking at the canned stew on his plate. "Only about the things I don't like."

"Which seems to me to be just about everything."

"Well, you sure don't cook as good as Mom does," his son said. "She knows what I like."

Fred held his temper and let the comment pass. These domestic things were the ones that got to him the most, he knew, because they made him feel inadequate. It wasn't that he couldn't do them; he just didn't do them with the grace and ease that Karen did. And the children always picked up on it. Always.

In fact, everyone seemed to pick up on it, often treating him as though being wifeless and being helpless were the same thing. Everyone, that is, except those fellow police officers who were still bachelors. Most of them treated him as though he were a dog let off a leash and assumed that all he wanted was "action." Well, he didn't, and those few times he had let himself be talked into blind dates had all been disasters. People meant well, but they sure didn't seem to understand the kind of transition he was going through. Not that he could blame them; he wasn't sure he understood it himself.

In contrast to the stew, his dessert—a doughnut with a scoop of vanilla ice cream and butterscotch sauce—was a unanimous success. After they'd finished, Nat and Sharon got ready for bed while he washed up in the kitchenette. Just as he was finishing, he heard a disagreement starting up; so, taking a deep breath, he went to see what was going on.

"Why can't I ever sleep in the big bed with you?" Sharon complained as he entered the bedroom.

"Because I'm the oldest," Nat interrupted, "and I get to sleep with Dad, that's why."

"Okay, okay, just a minute here," Fred said, sitting on the edge of the bed.

"He always gets to. It's not fair!" Sharon went over to her father and clambered up onto his lap. "Please, Daddy? Can I this time?"

"It has nothing at all to do with being older," Fred told her firmly. "It's just the way it works in families. When there aren't enough beds to go around, the daughters sleep with the mothers and the sons sleep with the fathers. If Mom were here, you'd get to sleep with her in the big bed and Nat would sleep on the cot. All right?" He gave her a squeeze. "Now let's get going. We've got a whole Parcheesi game to get through before bedtime."

As they set up the pieces, Fred sneaked a glance at his watch. Only forty minutes to go, he thought a little guiltily. There sure are satisfactions to being a parent, but no wonder Mother Nature arranged things so that there'd usually be two!

\* \* \*

I found Fred's story painful, and I told him so. He looked surprised.

"I sensed so many different emotions coming from you as you talked," I explained. "Loneliness, uncertainty, strain, grief . . . love. . . ."

"You're batting a thousand so far," he said. "I know that's one reason it's hard for me to have the kids around: I get churned up in so many different ways. It does hurt. It is painful."

"But not all the time."

"Uh-uh. Sometimes it feels real good."

"You know," I began uncertainly, "you said you thought you needed the kids more than they needed you. I'm wondering about that."

"I just meant that I miss them a lot. And yes, I am lonely a lot of the time. They don't seem sad when it's time for them to go back to Karen. But I feel sad. Every time. I understand they don't mind going . . . going home. They have a good life there with lots to do, and Karen's a good mother."

His voice trailed off. I knew that even thinking about those times had given him a lump in his throat.

"Can't we get out of here?" I asked. "You must at least have some coffee at your place."

"Yeah, I've got coffee. I live on coffee. But the apartment is a mess. That's one good thing about having the kids over. It makes me clean up the place before they come."

I said nothing, and neither, for a long moment, did Fred. "Okay," he said, "but don't say I didn't warn you."

It was untidy, and the apartment itself was pretty shabby. Harsh overhead lighting didn't make it any cozier. Just before Fred closed the bedroom door, I glimpsed an unmade bed, a pile of laundry on the floor and, incongruously, a crisp police uniform on a hanger on the closet door—an elegant scarecrow in a field gone to seed.

As Fred put the water on to boil and got out the mugs and a jar of instant coffee, I tried to recapture my train of thought.

"About the kids needing you. . . . You don't really believe they *don't* need you, do you?"

"They love me, I know that. But I don't know if they need me."

"It seems obvious to me that boys and girls do need fathers," I said. "Surely the needs that children have for fathering are different from—but just as important as—their needs for mothering. Don't you think that was true in your case? I'm sure it was in mine."

"I guess I loved my mom and dad in different ways," he admitted. "Still do, come to think of it. But I sure couldn't tell you why or how."

"I don't think any of us could. But I know I'd have felt...incomplete somehow if one of them hadn't been around at all."

"Yeah. Mom hasn't been too well lately. I'm going to feel kind of empty if anything happens to her...even at my age."

"That's what I mean. The kids need you to be their father, even if it's tough sometimes. And you *are* their father. Being a father is part of being who you are. You need the kids around from time to time to let you be that. Of course I'm a fine one to talk, since I'm blissfully single!"

He snorted at the phrase. Setting down two mugs of coffee, he gestured around the apartment. "Tell me what's blissful! You sound just like those guys at work who treat me like the only bull in a cow pasture. It seems like everyone has a lonely sister or a wife with lonely friends these days. I'm supposed to go after them all. And you know why?"

"Because they think it would be good for you, I suppose."

"You got it. And it isn't. They've even got me wondering if there's something wrong with me."

"That happens to a lot of people after a death."

He looked at me, puzzled.

"Let's say a husband dies. All the widow's well-meaning friends start ransacking the cupboards for eligible males to take his place. Almost immediately. I don't know why people can't understand that after a loss we need time to grieve, and time to work through that grief, before we can start making new relationships."

"What no one seems to understand about this whole thing, Will, is that although I want to get out of my marriage, I'm not happy to get out of my marriage. It makes me feel awful—about Karen, about the kids, about myself. I didn't want this to happen. I *don't* want it to happen! So why am I doing it? Because I know that for the past couple of years Karen and I have been slowly killing each other. It's going to get worse if we go on.

"The kids could get really screwed up living with parents like that. I can't ever be the person Karen wants me to be. She'll never be able to be who she wants to be as long as I'm around . . . and that goes for me, too. So the way I see it, we've all got to go through this really lousy period in order to make it all come out better in the end."

"It means working through a whole lot of strong feelings along the way, doesn't it?"

Fred nodded. "And it's lonely. God knows, it's lonely. Lots of people want to try to help, but you wouldn't believe how often their 'help' is worse than no help at all. I rely on Gloria a lot. I don't know what I'd do without her."

"I wanted to ask you about her. Where's she living now?"

"Just out in Edgewood with her family. Her girls are almost grown up now. Ellen's sixteen, and Anne's about to turn fourteen. They're great, too. I don't know if you remember: Gloria married Ralph Houck. He's a school superintendent and a hell of a nice guy. I spend a lot of time over there."

"You're lucky to have them. I was even thinking of giving her a call one of these days."

"You should do that. We were all out at Mom and Dad's the other day and they said you'd stopped by. Gloria wondered what had become of you."

We talked a little longer about this and that—people we'd known, things we'd done, past times. What I remember most is that by the end of the evening any tension between us had disappeared. We were back to being buddies again. I felt good about that on the drive home, and it suddenly occurred to me why it had happened. Somewhere along the way, I had stopped trying to be a pastoral counselor—and Fred had probably forgotten that I was a minister. Funny how being known as a professional helper sometimes gets in the way of helping.

Had I let Fred down by settling for the more comfortable "buddy" status? No. Once again, the important thing was that I had been myself, and the more I thought about it, the more I realized that being a friend *is* one way of being a minister.

# SCENE SEVEN: MID-SEPTEMBER

Knowing how quickly time can slip by, I made a note on my calendar to call Gloria the following week. I had the easy excuse of having just seen Fred, and I made no bones about my real curiosity. I was involved with the Lynches, and I wanted to know how their relatives and friends were reacting to their separation. Could we get together?

Even over the telephone I could tell that Gloria hadn't changed—except, perhaps, to become more the way she used to be. "I talk best over food," she insisted good-naturedly and then went on to fix the date, the restaurant, and the time. I felt a twinge of irritation at her assumption that I probably had nothing else planned for that day. I even had the petty temptation to say I couldn't do it then, just to be assertive in response. As it happened, her suggestion was a convenient one, and so I agreed.

She hadn't changed much physically, either, except to become more mature and better looking. She seemed to have grown into her height—Gloria must be about 5'10"— and while she once tended toward the gangly and slightly stooped posture of the uncertain young adult, she now sailed into the restaurant looking positively Junoesque in a light blue suit with matching brown bag, shoes, and belt. Her dark hair was slightly bouffant and very becoming.

She seemed genuinely interested as she asked me about my parish and my work. Her questions were sensitive and perceptive. We talked, briefly, about her parents, and then she waded straight into the subject of our luncheon.

"Will," she said, "that was a bad marriage from the beginning. I knew Fred was making a mistake. I could kick myself for not telling him at the time."

"He wouldn't have heard you. Nobody ever does...."

"...when they're in love. I know. That's why I didn't bother. And there's always the chance you might be wrong, and then how do you undo the things you've said? Better not to say them. Better to let people make their own mistakes. I never got along with Karen, but then I wasn't marrying her and I wasn't going to have to live with her and her family.

"Anyway, there never was any feeling of wholeness about their marriage. They stayed two singles. Fred's real life was in his work, where he could be himself and Karen couldn't run things. At home she ran everything—her way. Fred was a pussycat. Sometimes he was almost like a child and Karen like his mother. Not, mind you, that she's anything like Mom! Then the kids came along, and once they weren't babies anymore Fred started wanting to be a father to them. Fathers are supposed to make decisions and deal with discipline and manage things, but all that sort of stuff had become Karen's job—because Fred had let it. So when he began to flex his muscles a little, he found himself wrestling with her. And he wasn't so happy at work anymore, either.

"It's been a bad scene in that house for almost two years now. If it was going to get resolved, it would have been resolved by now. I'm glad he still had the ability to stand up for himself and do something about it. But he's got a tough road ahead."

"Everyone has, I guess."

"Oh, sure, the divorce will take a toll on the four of them, and it's not easy on the rest of us who get dragged into it in one way or another. But I feel particularly sorry for Fred because he's given in to Karen for so long that he's almost lost his competence for daily living."

"How do you mean?"

"We all need some order and structure in our lives. She provided it for him. He can't do it on his own. For heaven's sake, you saw his place! You'd expect that kind of lifestyle from a college kid away from home for the first time, but not from a mature, adult individual with as much on the ball as Fred has."

"He told me how much of a help you were being to him."

"I try, I try. I think I'm going to drop my daughter Ellen down at his place one day a week. She could give it a good scrubbing, do the laundry, do the shopping.... Speaking of shopping, did Fred tell you about what happened when we took Sharon shopping last Saturday?"

Without waiting for my reply, she went right on and told me about it herself.

* * *

It was only because she knew it was Fred calling that Gloria got out of the shower to answer the phone. Brrrrrr, these mornings are cold now, she thought, as she ran across the hall holding onto her towel.

"Hello!" she said.

"Hi," he said. "It's me."

"Who else would it be when I'm in the shower?"

He chuckled. "It's the only time I can be sure of finding you at home."

"What's up?"

"Got a problem. Sharon wants a corduroy jumper. What's it going to cost, and where should I go to get it?"

"May all your problems be such important ones! Oh, I'd say about eight or ten dollars. That's at a discount store. It'll cost more downtown. Karen would know the best place to find Sharon's size. My girls are practically into my clothes these days."

"Karen's told Sharon to forget it. She doesn't think a jumper is ... uh ... suitable. So I'm going to get one for her instead."

"Is that the voice of generosity or spite?"

"Hey, hey, I just asked you for some advice! I'll keep it at my place and Sharon can wear it on weekends."

"You didn't answer my question."

"Look. . . ."

"Okay, okay, I'm sorry. Tell you what: Why don't the three of us go shopping this Saturday morning? Ralph's got to work, and Ellen and Anne can watch Nathan. They'd love it."

"Thought you'd never ask," Fred said. "What time do you want us to show up?"

"How about ten?"

"Fine. That'll give me a chance to clean this place up a bit."

"As I recall, it could use it. . . . But count me out on that one," Gloria said. "I've got my hands full right here, thank you very much."

"I wasn't suggesting. . . ."

"I know, dear brother. I was just joking. Don't be so defensive."

Fred sighed and there was a short silence.

"I'm standing here freezing," Gloria said. "Saturday at ten?"

"Sure, that'll be good. Thanks."

"And try to be roughly on time, okay?"

"Okay," he said and hung up.

It was 10:15 on Saturday morning when Gloria heard a car door slam and the shouts of Nathan and Sharon as they ran up the front walk. She greeted them outside and gave Fred a hug.

"Want to come in for a minute?" she asked.

"I'll just say 'hi' to Ellen and Anne and then we can get going. What time do you guess we'll be back?"

"Oh, three . . . three-thirty, maybe."

"You've got to be kidding! All that time for one jumper?"

"Welcome to harsh reality," she laughed. "Driving and hunting . . . and lunch. . . ." She shrugged. "Who knows?"

It's just like Fred to think he can get something like this done in a minute, she thought. Everyone talks about how hard it's been for women to adjust to the demands of the marketplace, but what about men who have to learn the facts of domesticity? Brother!

They searched through two shopping malls miles apart from each other, tried a children's specialty shop in yet a third suburb, and decided over lunch to give up and head to a downtown department store. It was there that Sharon emerged, beaming, from a fitting cubicle. "This one, Daddy. This is the one I want. This very one."

"What do you think?" Fred asked Gloria.

She walked around Sharon, surveying her up and down. "I think it's skimpy. It looks too tight. It'll probably shrink some. She'll grow out of it in a week. It's $17.50. . . ."

Sharon interrupted. "It's just what I want," she insisted. "It's got a pocket and buttons and straps like Beth's. Please?" Her voice had taken on a whine, and her hands stroked the front of the jumper.

"You sure they don't have the next size up?" Fred asked.

Gloria shook her head.

"Okay, we'll take it," Fred decided.

"Good lord," Gloria said with a sigh as Sharon hopped in a circle and clapped her hands. "What a pushover!"

"If it's what she wants," Fred said. He turned to his daughter. "Now go take it off so we can get out of here."

"You might as well let her wear it home," Gloria said. "It may not fit by the time we get there."

On their way through the store to the parking ramp, Sharon stopped at a table and grabbed a pair of brown fur-lined boots. "Hey!" she called to Fred and Gloria, who were walking on ahead. "Can I have these, too?"

Fred came back to look. "You've got boots, haven't you?" he asked.

"But not like these. Beth has some like these."

"Look, honey," Fred began, "they're awfully expensive, and. . . ."

"My boots are too little. Mommy said so. She said you'd buy me some."

"I'll talk it over with your mother the next time I see her," Fred said.

"Oh, please, Daddy?"

Gloria walked back to where they were standing. "You heard what your father said, Sharon. He'll talk it over with your mother and see what sort of boots you need. Come on, now."

"I want boots like this," Sharon said, her bottom lip pushing out defiantly.

Fred stood by silently.

"Look," Gloria continued. "Your dad's just bought you an expensive new jumper and now you're getting all pouty because he won't buy you expensive new boots you don't even need."

"I do so!"

"Stop acting like a spoiled brat. Put them down. Let's go." Fred and Gloria resumed their walk to the ramp, with Sharon dawdling along behind. Once they were in the car, she sat in the back seat staring out the window and saying nothing.

Fred and Gloria talked about Christmas vacation plans and tried to decide how their children could spend some time together. Then their conversation shifted to the school Sharon had just entered that fall.

"Do you still like it?" Gloria asked, looking over her shoulder at her niece.

Sharon responded with a shrug. Gloria held out her hand toward her and said, "Come on, Sharon, how about being friends again?" Then, noticing a bright green coin purse in her hand, she added, "Say, that's pretty. Did your mother give it to you?"

Sharon nodded.

"Anything in it?"

Sharon shook her head.

"Well, we'll have to fix that!" Gloria said cheerfully, taking it and rummaging in her bag for change. "There," she said, extracting two quarters. She snapped open the little purse.

It wasn't empty after all. It contained some tissue paper and a price tag from the store they'd just left.

"Oh, boy," she breathed.

Fred glanced at her inquiringly.

"It looks like we forgot to pay for something." She turned back to her niece. "Sharon, tell me the truth. Where did you get this purse?"

Sharon stared at her blankly.

"Sharon, Aunt Gloria asked you a question. Answer her," Fred said.

When Sharon still remained silent, Fred pulled off the road and turned to face his daughter. Tears were welling up in her eyes.

Fred examined the purse. "You took it from the store, didn't you?"

Sharon began to whimper.

"That's called stealing," Fred continued, his voice rising, "and you know it! What's gotten into you, anyway? I can tell you one thing, young lady, we're going right back to the store and you're going to apologize to the clerk. And if you weren't already wearing your jumper, I'd take that back, too! You're lucky you're only five or they'd lock you up!" The tires squealed as he did a U-turn. By now Sharon was sobbing uncontrollably.

Gloria tried to quell the uneasy feeling that she was in some way responsible, too. "You know, it's not grand larceny," she said quietly to her brother.

"It's stealing, whatever you want to call it," Fred declared angrily. He glared at his daughter in the rear-view mirror. "You know what I ought to do? I ought to tan your hide, that's what. If you think any child of mine's going to grow up to be a shoplifter, you're wrong!"

When they reached the store, Fred pulled Sharon out of the car and marched her through the door. They were back in a moment. "Get in," he commanded, slamming the door after her.

Except for Sharon's ebbing sobs, they drove on in silence. After a few minutes, Gloria glanced into the back seat. Sharon appeared to be asleep, her thumb in her mouth.

Gloria could feel tension radiating from Fred like a force field. "Relax," she said. "It's all over."

Fred shook his head and took a deep breath. "No, it's not. It's only the beginning. Sharon would never have done that before. I can hear the delinquency counselor now: 'Typical child of a broken home.' That's what I'm going to have to live with."

Gloria watched the houses slip past, the trees, the children playing. "Yes and no, I guess," she said.

"That's not much help."

"What I mean is 'yes,' now that you've actually filed for divorce and are going through with it, you'll have to live with the suspicion that every bad thing Sharon and Nathan do is your fault because you split up the family. And 'no,' that isn't the way it is. Sure, Sharon's upset about her home coming apart, but other children swipe things, too. Mine did. Who grows up without problems?"

They pulled up in front of the house. "Want to come in?" Gloria asked.

Fred shook his head. "I'm pooped. Just send Nathan out. And tell him to be quiet because his sister's sleeping."

As Gloria opened her door to get out, Fred reached for her arm. "Thanks," he said. "I'm going to need you. So are the kids."

"Any time," she replied. "But try not to call when I'm in the shower, okay?"

He smiled, but she could see in his eyes all the pain and apprehension of facing an uncertain future.

*　*　*

Gloria finished her story with a slight hand gesture and nod of her head that seemed to say, "See what I mean?" What she actually said was, "Poor old Fred. He's such a lamb. And he tries hard. But he's really got a lot of pulling himself together to do."

-68-

"That's strange," I said. "He's always struck me as a very competent person. He's always done well at things, hasn't he?"

"Oh, yes, but in his own funny way. He's always been such an idealist, Will. He expected something out of college that he didn't find there, so that didn't work out even though he was a good student. Then deciding to be a cop . . . imagining, I suppose, that life would be like the little country community where we grew up. Anyone could have told him that working the city streets would be depressing and grubby. Then his marriage to Karen—I don't know what he hoped to find there, but once again he didn't find it. I wonder if he'll *ever* find what he's looking for."

"Don't we all go through some of that? The searching and the trying out, I mean."

Gloria shrugged. "Maybe it's different for a woman. Or at least a woman like me. I knew what I wanted, and I've got it. A solid husband I love, good kids, nice house, enough money. I don't work, I enjoyed growing up with my kids, and now I keep plenty busy doing things that I want to do. Maybe I was lucky. Maybe I'm not very imaginative. Maybe a lot of things. But I'm happy."

"How do you think Nat and Sharon are taking it?"

"They're okay. It has to be confusing and upsetting for them, traveling back and forth from their mom to their dad and getting used to not having Fred at home. But kids cope. Nat and Sharon are well looked after. I'm not saying it's not hard for them, but they'll get used to it. I mean, really, what choice do they have? No, it's Fred I worry about the most."

"He's still your kid brother, isn't he?"

She thought that over for a moment before asking, "Don't you think he needs a big sister right now?"

"I'm sure he does."

"No, you're not. I can tell."

"I *am* sure he needs a sister, Gloria, and I meant it when I said he and the kids were lucky to have you around. I guess I was just wondering how 'big' that sister needs to be. People sometimes have a way of becoming incompetent when other people expect them to be. We both know that Fred is a perfectly able person. Maybe he needs help in feeling that he is."

"I sometimes wonder if he is able."

"Seriously?"

"Well, semi-seriously, anyway."

"I just find myself worrying more about how Nat and Sharon will get through all this than about how Fred will. I'll bet *they* need to feel their father's competent and in charge."

"There's not much I can do about that, is there?" she asked.

"When you're with them, you might be able to find ways to let them know you think he is, that he's their father and he's the one who makes the decisions. Even if you don't think his decisions are the right ones.

"I can't help thinking of one family *I* tried to help several years ago. The husband had started his own small construction business and was killed in a building accident. There were four kids. The oldest was twelve. The wife was paralyzed by her grief and overwhelmed by the demands of her children and the paperwork that had to be sorted out. Yet, underneath it all, she was a very bright and capable woman.

"Anyway," I went on, "I found someone to live in with her, and we organized people to bring food, and I got one of my parishioners who was a lawyer to give her that kind of help, and I felt really good about what we were able to do for that family. The only problem was that the wife went into a deep depression and one of the kids—the four-year-old—started becoming unmanageable, acting out, wetting her bed. It went on for months, and the more we did, the worse it seemed to get. Finally we were smart enough to call for help from a family crisis center, and little by little they were able to help that mother regain some confidence in her own ability to cope. We'd been telling her, in actions if not in words, that we didn't think she could—and she'd believed us. As she got stronger, her little daughter seemed to share that growing strength, and her problems let up, too.

"I guess what I'm saying is that in the urge to be helpful we can sometimes make people helpless. But it's not an easy line to draw, that's for sure."

Gloria toyed with her coffee cup. "I've wondered about professional help for Fred. Maybe that's the answer. Only it seems such an admission of defeat. You know what I mean?"

"Sure. A lot of people feel that way. But I've learned that it's the strong, not the weak, who can ask for help when they need it."

Our check arrived. I offered to pick it up, but at Gloria's insistence we split it down the middle. "Otherwise," she explained, "we'll have to try and remember whose turn it is next time. And Will," she added, "let's be sure there *is* a next time."

"I'd like that," I said, and with that we left—she to a board meeting for some good cause, and I to my work.

Somewhere in my conversations with Abe Lewi, he had mentioned the depression that would-be helpers can feel when they find themselves stymied in their desire to help. Talking with Gloria had brought into focus another piece of the helping puzzle: the depression that helpers can inadvertently trigger in the people they're trying to help.

I thought a lot about those two negative outcomes of a positive urge, wondering what clues they provided that might lead to a definition of constructive helping. Both certainly pointed to the necessity of helping people help themselves rather than trying to solve their problems for them. I pondered for a while and finally came up with something I was comfortable with: Constructive helping involves allowing and encouraging a person to maintain a sense of self and self-worth. That means supporting the *person* no matter how he or she chooses to find a way through life's tangles.

The day after Gloria and I had lunch together, I got a call from Abe Lewi inviting me to a cocktail party at his house—a farewell party. He and his family were moving to Houston, where he was going to work at a new psychiatric center for children.

"There'll be some colleagues of mine you might like to meet," he said. "And why don't you come early, before the others? It'll be our last chance to catch up." I told him I'd be delighted to accept.

When Saturday night rolled around, it was still warm enough to sit out on the Lewis' back porch, and that's where Abe and I talked. I found him to be full of ambivalence about his move. There were, of course, all the problems of schools and housing and change of climate and cost of living, not to mention the general hassle of moving. What bothered him most was having to uproot secure ties to friends and workmates. For his wife, the move was going to mean the loss of her piano students, a lengthy period without income, the chores of building a new nest, and probably several years before she would be back to exactly where she was right now.

"So tell me something *good* about the move," I begged.

"Growth," he said. "Personal and professional growth. Now there's a good, trite phrase that's meant to justify just about anything. What can I tell you? I'm really excited about the people who are coming together at this new facility. It's precisely the kind of work I want to be doing—and it offers me the chance to be a shaping force. There's the prestige. And more money which, naturally, won't go far down there and will be eaten up by inflation. But all the same, it's a new place with new faces."

"A whole new . . . tangle," I said. He gave me a quizzical look, but I didn't explain. "I find myself envying you. Why? Why do these chances to take our old selves into new situations make our hearts beat a little faster?"

"It's not true for everyone. Some people find new circumstances threatening and upsetting. I don't really know. Maybe it's partly genetic. It probably has something to do with the very, very early process of personality development, with the origins of curiosity and creativity. Incidentally, my special area of research is going to be the first year of life. How could I say no to *that* chance?"

He turned the talk to me and my work, showing genuine curiosity in what I was hearing and seeing—and particularly in what I was making of it all. When I brought him up to date on the Lynch-Sawyer situation and relayed to him the doubts Fred had expressed about being needed by his children, Abe set off on a discourse that was, for him, unusually vehement.

"How right you were to reinforce his role as father!" he exclaimed. "It often happens that the noncustodial parent relinquishes the parenting role, and there are real pressures and understandable reasons why this happens. In your friend's case, the time he has with his children is limited. He wants that time to be special and good and happy. Who wouldn't?

"But I know, as most parents know, that the parenting function means more than just making the children happy. It also means setting limits and making decisions during those years when children aren't capable of doing these things on their own. This creates a healthy tension, although it may not always seem healthy and may in fact cause periods of stress and conflict between the parent and the children. Some noncustodial parents try to avoid this stress and conflict. They need to be reminded that setting limits is an important way for parents to express their love and concern for their children. It's a big part of parenting.

"My feelings are that the noncustodial person should be just as much a parent as the custodial one. As you pointed out, a child's needs for mothering are different from a child's needs for fathering. A child needs both. When friends and relatives start building obstacles between the children of a divorce and one of the parents, they are doing a tremendous disservice to those children. I'm not talking about those instances in which one of the parents represents a potential danger to the children. I'm talking about the great majority of divorces. In them the separation occurs because of irreconcilable differences between the adults, and yet each adult is still perfectly capable of parenting."

"So what you're saying is that one parent can't be both mother and father," I commented. "At least not successfully."

"I'm not sure that we'd be able to define 'successfully.' Up to a point, each parent does have to both mother and father when he or she is alone with the children for long periods of time. In some ways neither one can be both. I think that's part of the strain of being a single parent."

He leaned back and looked up at the evening sky. "Look at it this way: A single parent has nothing tangible against which to define his or her role. If your friend, Fred, were still living with Karen, he'd probably be much more comfortable in providing a male role model—in providing the masculine identification for his children. With trusted partners, mothers and fathers can be more secure in their roles than when they're on their own. But can a child grow up 'successfully' with a single parent? Of course. Millions have."

"With lots of strains of their own."

"Well, sure. Often strains that are deep and subtle and lasting but not necessarily debilitating. Who grew up without strain? It's a necessary part of the process of becoming who we are. But, yes, growing up with a single parent does produce its own tensions . . . like Sharon wanting to sleep with her father. . . ."

"I was thinking, after I talked to Fred, that he could have solved the whole problem by putting another mattress on the floor for Nat so that neither child slept in bed with him."

Abe shook his head. "It wouldn't have made any difference. Sharon would still have wanted to sleep with her dad. You see, these things often look like sibling rivalry, but they're not. Five-year-old girls often want to sleep with their fathers. They just plain want to. But in addition to that want, there's also fear—particularly in the absence of a mother who occupies that place or generally intercepts her young daughter's sexual feelings toward her father.

"Don't misunderstand me, Will," Abe went on. "It's the healthiest and most natural thing in the world for fathers to cuddle their little daughters. Physical affection of that kind is a really important element of a young girl's emotional development. If we're lucky we can all remember snuggling into bed with our parents when we needed to— when we didn't feel well, or when we were scared, or just for the sheer joy of it on a Saturday morning.

"That kind of fathering isn't what I'm concerned about at all. In Sharon's case I'm thinking about a very young girl who, by circumstance, is thrown into uncertainty about who the 'Mommy' is in Daddy's life now that her Mommy doesn't live with him anymore. Deep down inside she may be wondering, 'Could it be me?' That possibility would have to be both exciting and overwhelming at Sharon's age when it's awfully hard to handle that amount of feeling by yourself. Wanting to take Mommy's place in Daddy's bed would be one way of asking that question. Fred's response let her know that he loved her as a daughter and that being a *daughter* was her special place in the family. That may have been very helpful to her right then."

I thought of Fred's repeated references to loneliness. "How hard it must be for one parent to be suddenly isolated from that tightly interwoven unit! To be all alone would have to be traumatic, even though the marriage weren't a happy one."

Abe nodded sympathetically. "In reality, you know, it's seldom a *two* unit that gets split into two isolated *ones*. Each half of the couple has always had multiple other attachments—for instance, to kin and friends. When a divorce occurs, certain aspects of the couple's bonding no longer exist while a lot of other aspects are still present. With time, some continuing ones will strengthen and some will weaken. And there will be new ones. Just because the partners split doesn't mean that they go into isolation from everyone else."

"The children of the divorce stay part of those multiple attachments, too."

"You bet. And they need to. That's why the quality of those continuing extended relationships can make so much difference in the way those children will weather the storm."

"I know," I said. "I'm really coming to appreciate that. And in that regard, I wish I could feel better about Gloria's relationship with Fred and the children. For all her good intentions, it made me very uneasy . . . the way she seemed so ready to move in as wife and mother."

"What I heard in your telling of it," said Abe, "was her willingness to be wife-mother to *Fred*. I didn't hear that she felt at all maternal toward Sharon. Gloria's got a lot to deal with—her hostility toward Karen; her past and present feelings and fantasies about her brother; her feelings about her own marriage and children. She's just like all of us: One point of tension pulls on a lot of different strings.

"And Sharon's regressive behavior was almost guaranteed to be anxiety-producing under the circumstances—wanting that jumper, maybe hoping that soon it wouldn't fit so she could demand another one, wanting boots like her friend's. That's pretty overt behavior for a five-year-old. Even though she's been bought a bunch of stuff, she feels deprived. Because she *is* deprived—emotionally deprived. So she steals something to make up for what's lost—something symbolic of her mother.

"People tend to get very anxious in the presence of regressive behavior, particularly in children. That's strange, in a way, because kids should be free to regress periodically and feel comfortable doing so. But adult anxiety often comes out as anger and resentment. Too bad."

The doorbell rang. "Here comes the party," he said. "Ready to be social?"

"Sure," I said. "I'm looking forward to it. And thanks, Abe, for the many chances to talk."

"I hope we'll go on talking even across greater distances," he said, getting to his feet. "Not in the search for more answers," he added with a laugh, "but in search of better questions." He gave my arm a squeeze as we entered the house. "We may never get to know the 'right' things to do," he said. "In these kinds of situations, the dynamics of each family, even as it comes apart, are unique. Perhaps all any outsider can do is to offer as much constructive, nonjudgmental support as possible."

# Scene Eight: November

I didn't see much of the Lynches or the Sawyers during October, and my parishioners kept me pretty busy. I performed two weddings and three baptisms—duties which to me are always joyful. Then the holiday season was approaching, and I started gearing up for Thanksgiving and Christmas.

On the Sunday before Thanksgiving, Karen Lynch and her mother came to church together. I noticed them during the reading of the First Lesson, and the effect their presence had on me told me something about my own inward journeys: I felt a sense of calmness.

I almost said "serenity," but that seems a bit strong to describe the occasion. I know that part of my calmness came from a feeling of confidence that I was providing a service, in both senses of the word, which I was properly equipped and qualified to provide. I was in my right place—not acting as amateur psychologist but as minister—making available something of fineness and beauty, optimism and hope, promise, comfort, and compassion . . . and discipline. Yes, that too.

But it was not just I, Will Morgan, who was giving these things, any more than a plate-glass window gives the sun that shines through it. For whatever reason Karen and Virginia were there—whether they were seeking warmth or illumination—they would get it not from me but from the faith I represented. That would be the source of healing for them.

As we sang the closing hymn, I thought back to the last time I'd seen Karen. It had been in May, over six months ago. Then she'd told me that she felt she didn't "belong" in the church anymore because she was single again. That's a fairly common feeling among separated and divorced people, and I hadn't pushed any further discussion of it. I was glad she'd made the effort to come back and wondered what had changed her mind.

Mother and daughter stayed for the coffee hour, and even before I could go over and tell them how welcome they were, they came over to me.

"That was a lovely service, Will, and thank you," Karen said.

"Why, it's really the first social event Karen's been to since all the trouble started," her mother confided. "I've been telling her that she has to keep up her friendships, but of course it's not easy. I thought she might need a little moral support today, so here we are."

So Karen had come at her mother's prompting. Well, at least she had come.

"It's not as hard as I thought it would be," Karen said. "All the same," she added, "it is difficult for me not to feel that I'm being judged."

I nodded. "This is no judgment seat," I said. "Meanwhile, we all need all the love and support we can find. That's what I hope you'll find here."

"Will," Virginia said, laying a hand on my arm, "of course Dwight Lynch hasn't had a chance to call you, but I'm sure he'd want you to know that Ruth had a minor heart attack on Thursday. She's in Montefiore Hospital under observation."

"How serious is it?" I asked.

"They don't seem to think it was terribly serious at all," Virginia said. "She was in intensive care only overnight and is quite stable and comfortable now."

I started to ask how long they expected Ruth to be in the hospital, but our conversation was interrupted by a familiar bright young voice at my elbow.

"Hi, Mrs. Lynch, Mrs. Sawyer!" It was Nancy Quinn, one of my choristers and a great help around the church.

"I didn't know you all knew each other," I said.

"Know Nancy?" said Mrs. Sawyer. "Why, she's Karen's prize babysitter! I don't know what she'd do without her."

"And Nat and Sharon's favorite," said Karen. "They're really lucky to have her."

"They're wonderful kids, Mrs. Lynch," Nancy said, "and that's more than I can say about some of the little tigers I look after from time to time."

I excused myself, leaving the three of them chatting. As the room cleared and I was getting ready to go back to my office, Nancy sought me out.

"Can we talk for a moment, Reverend Morgan?" she asked.

"Sure," I said. "Come along with me. What's up?"

As we walked down the hall together, Nancy explained that while what she had said was true—she did enjoy babysitting for Karen Lynch and genuinely liked Nat and Sharon—her evenings there were getting difficult.

"I'm sure they are," I said, opening the door to my office and motioning her inside. "That's a hard job when there's trouble in a family."

She hopped up and perched on the windowsill. "It's like . . . like I don't know what to say or do sometimes, and I'm real scared of doing the wrong thing."

"There isn't always a 'right' thing to do, Nancy. Often we just do what we can."

"Sure. But I mean there can still be a 'wrong' thing to do. Like Friday evening . . . we were watching something on TV and Nat suddenly asked me, 'Is Nana going to die?' I didn't know what the right answer was, but it really scared me because I was sure there were lots of wrong ones."

"What did you tell him?"

"I said: 'No, Nat, she's going to be just fine. You'll see, she'll be back home in no time.' But, Reverend Morgan, what if she isn't? What happens if she does die?"

I paused a bit. "I don't know what I'd have said to Nat. Maybe I'd have tried something like: 'You know, Nat, everything that is alive will die one day. But I don't think your grandmother is going to die right now. The doctors and nurses will help her live as long as she possibly can.' Something like that, perhaps. Then you wouldn't have had to sound like you were making a promise."

She thought about that for a moment. "You know, I did make another promise to Nat not long ago, and I don't feel good about that one, either, because I can't tell his mother about it."

"Do you feel like telling me?"

She nodded. "Maybe you can help me figure out how to handle this whole thing."

* * *

"That's really sad about the Lynches," Nancy's roommate said. "I'll bet you were hoping they'd get back together. And the kids are so cute! What do you say to them when they talk about it?"

Nancy finished gathering up her books and papers, stuffing them into a tote bag. "They don't," she said, and added, "Thank heavens! I don't know what I'd say. Yeah, you're right about hoping they'd get back together. But I guess once a divorce is filed, it's time to stop hoping." She sat on the edge of her bed. "Sally . . . how old were you when your folks got divorced?"

"Seven."

"How did you feel about it?"

"Awful. I thought it was all my fault; that they were fighting about me all the time."

"Did you have anyone you could talk to?"

Sally shook her head. "Being a military brat, every time I really got to like somebody, we moved. After a while I didn't even *want* to make friends."

"Some life!"

"Yeah, but we survived, more or less. When you look around at the kids here at school, you can see there are all kinds of ways to grow up. There's sure no recipe for success!"

Nancy laughed. "I guess not. You going out tonight?"

"Uh-uh. Too much homework to do."

She got up to leave. "I'll see you later, then. I won't be late."

She walked along the campus paths in the afternoon light, under the trees that were almost bare now and past the orderly buildings with their blue-and-white identification signs planted in the leaf-strewn grass. She wondered what Sally's childhood had really been like. All that travel . . . all that upset. And what a great person! As for me, she thought, here I am farther away from home than I've ever been before—a big 500 miles! Wow! With Mom and Dad still in the same house where we were all born. . . .

Karen Lynch met her at the door.

"Sharon should be waking up," she said. "I've got to run. Mrs. Geary's number is by the phone, and I'll be back by their bedtime. Leftovers are in the refrigerator. All you have to do is heat 'em up. Everything okay with you?"

"Fine," Nancy said. "Don't worry about a thing."

"You're great," Karen said. "Just make yourself at home, like always! 'Bye!" With a wave, she hurried out to the car.

Nancy could hear a pounding in the cellar. Nathan, she guessed, building something, as usual. She tiptoed upstairs and looked into Sharon's room. The child was tossing fretfully, so Nancy walked over and squatted down beside her.

"Sharon?" she said softly.

The girl's tossing ceased. Her eyelids fluttered and half opened. Still between sleep and waking, Sharon stared at Nancy, then frowned and broke into tears.

"Hey, honey, it's me. What's the matter?"

Sharon only cried harder. Nancy sat on the bed and reached over to smooth her hair. "Were you having a bad dream or something?"

Sharon nodded.

"Well, it's okay now. There's nothing to be afraid of."

The girl's crying lessened. "Mommy . . .," she said.

"Your mom's gone out for a while. She'll be back by bedtime. You want to go to the playground and then help me make supper?"

The crying stopped. Sharon thought for a moment and then nodded again. "Will you push me real high on the swings?"

"As high as you like," Nancy said, stroking the girl's cheek. "Feel better now?"

Sharon sat up and leaned her head against Nancy's shoulder. "I guess so," she said. "I hate scary dreams."

"I do, too," Nancy agreed. "But it's sort of a nice feeling when you wake up and realize that it was only a dream. Come on, then. Get your shoes and socks on and we'll go play. I'll see if Nat's ready."

When they came within sight of the playground, Nathan ran on ahead. "Careful!" Nancy shouted. She stayed close to Sharon, who was inspecting an anthill.

"Do ants have mommies and daddies?" Sharon asked.

Nancy hesitated. "I guess they do. Sort of. I think mommy ants lay eggs like chickens and the baby ants are in the eggs."

"Then ants don't need daddies at all," said Sharon.

"Oh, yes, they do," Nancy said, feeling a surge of panic. "Isn't it funny how they all walk in lines when they leave their anthill?"

"Why do they need daddies?"

"They need daddies because . . .," oh, lord, she thought. "They need daddies because . . . it's the daddies who put the baby ants in the eggs. Otherwise the eggs would be empty." That's done it, she thought. What now?

But no more questions came. Sharon poked at the line of ants and then suddenly jumped up and ran after her brother. Nancy followed, vastly relieved.

Nathan didn't use the swings for swinging. Instead, he climbed up one side of the frame and hung by his hands from the crossbar. Then, hand over hand, he made his way over to the other side.

"Hey, that's neat!" Nancy shouted. "When did you learn to do that?"

"Oh, I can do lots of things!" Nathan shouted back. "Watch this!" Nathan again climbed the frame. This time he sat on the top of the crossbar and lowered himself backwards very slowly until his knees were locked over the bar. Then he let go with his hands.

"Great!" Nancy said, moving in close.

A little shakily, Nathan reached up for the bar, brought his legs off the bar and down under his chin, hung by his hands for a moment, and then dropped to the ground on all fours.

"Bravo!" Nancy said, clapping. "I didn't know you were that strong! I wouldn't want to try that. Who taught you all those tricks?"

"My dad," said Nathan, flushed and pleased with himself.

"My turn, my turn!" Sharon insisted, pulling at Nancy's arm. "You promised you'd swing me real high!"

Back home again, they made supper and then settled down to watch television. Nathan, who usually provided a running commentary, was quiet. Nancy noticed that he was more absorbed in playing with a toy motorcycle on the arm of the sofa than in watching the program.

During a commercial, the telephone rang. It was Karen calling to ask if Nancy could stay later than they'd agreed; she and Diane wanted to go to a movie.

"No problem," Nancy said, "I've got tons of work to do. Whenever you get home'll be fine."

"Thanks, Nancy, you're a doll," Karen said. "Everything okay with the kids?"

"Uh-huh. We're just about to get ready for bed."

"Give them a hug for me and tell them I'll see them in the morning, okay?"

"You bet," Nancy said.

Later that evening, as she pored over her psychology textbook, Nancy heard a sound upstairs. The kids had been in bed for almost an hour and should have been asleep by now. She listened for a moment, decided that it must have been her imagination, and then definitely heard a door softly close.

Going up to investigate, she first checked on Sharon. The door was open, the room dark, but she could see Sharon's head on her pillow and hear her steady breathing. At the end of the corridor, Nathan's door was shut and there was a line of light underneath it. She knocked on the door and opened it when she got no response. Nathan was sitting in the middle of the floor, methodically packing a small suitcase.

"Nathan!" she exclaimed. "What on earth are you doing?"

He looked up, pale and startled.

"What are you doing?" she repeated. "You're supposed to be in bed!"

"I'm packing," he said sullenly.

"Packing? Well . . . where do you think you're going? You don't go to your dad's for another three days!"

"Away," he said.

"Just 'away'?"

"I'm going to run away. And no one's going to stop me." He stuffed a tee shirt into the case.

"Hey, Nat, this is serious. Did I do something to make you mad?"

Nathan shook his head.

"Is it . . . is it your mom and dad?"

He nodded.

"Do you want to talk about it?"

He shrugged.

Nancy took a deep breath. "Oh, Nat," she said, kneeling down beside him, "I wish I knew what to tell you! I'd be all upset, too. But think how your poor mom would worry if she came home and found you weren't here. She'd have to call the police, and everyone would have to start hunting for you, and we'd all be scared that something awful had happened. I'll bet your grandparents would have a fit! There are a lot of people around who love you, you know."

He didn't look at her but only frowned and toyed with the suitcase handle, lifting it up, dropping it down, lifting it up, dropping it down.

"At least couldn't you *wait* a while before running away?" she continued. "I mean, until things settle down a little bit? You can always run away if you really want to. It doesn't have to be tonight. It's cold now, too. If I ran away, I'd do it in summer...."

She was out of ideas, hoping desperately that she would hear the sound of the car pulling up outside; but all was quiet.

"Well...," Nat wavered, "maybe I'll wait for a while." Then, still not looking at her, he asked, "You going to tell my mom?"

She bit her lip. "No, Nat. I don't have to tell your mom."

"Promise?"

"If I promise, will you promise me something, too?"

Now he did look up at her, uncertain. "What?" he said.

"That when you *really* need to run away, you'll come tell me about it first. It'll be our secret, just between us."

He thought it over for a moment. "Okay," he said.

"Then we've got a deal?"

He nodded.

"Give me a hug," she said. He felt limp and tired in her arms. "Ready for bed now?" His head moved up and down against her shoulder.

Karen Lynch dropped her back at the dormitory. "Thanks, Nancy. I really mean it. Just getting away for an evening like that helps put everything back in perspective for a while."

"Any time, Mrs. Lynch," Nancy said. "I really enjoy being with your kids." She waved goodbye, hoping that Sally wasn't asleep yet so that she could talk it all over with someone.

*   *   *

"I've thought about it a lot since then, Reverend Morgan," Nancy said, "and I still don't know what would have been the right thing to do. But I don't feel good about keeping secrets from Mrs. Lynch. If Nat's so upset that he really wants to run away from home, someone should know about it, shouldn't they?"

I nodded. "You took a lot of responsibility by doing what you did. But that seemed the best way at the time to carry out your main responsibility, which was to keep Nat safe. And you succeeded. You can certainly feel good about that."

"I guess so."

"Perhaps the real question isn't so much what you should have done then, but rather what happens next. I mean, when you're babysitting Nat again, you might want to talk with him about that incident. You could ask him if he's thought any more about leaving home and see what he says. It's hard to deal with important things when they get buried and no one mentions them. Nat may need to talk about this with someone he trusts, and he sure seems to trust you."

"But it will still be a secret."

"When you talk to him, you may find a way to change that."

"I'll try, Reverend Morgan," Nancy said, easing herself off of the windowsill. "I still wish I knew what would have been the right thing to do at the time."

"Life's chock-full of times like that. Generally, we just end up doing the best we can. Let me think about it, though, and we'll talk again. All right?"

"You bet," she said. "I'll be thinking about it, too."

## SCENE NINE: DECEMBER

I had a chance to talk to Nancy again on Wednesday when she came over for choir practice after school, and we had what I think was a fruitful conversation. What I remember most was our discussion of how easy it is for people who work with children to slip in between them and their parents—without, of course, meaning to.

Nancy clearly enjoyed children and readily admitted that she was both pleased and flattered by the special relationships she had been able to form with several of the children for whom she babysat. In most instances, she and the children in her care had their own games and jokes and rituals. She was surprised at how many of her friends seemed to have problems when they went out babysitting. While she was talking about that she said something, almost casually, that explained a great deal: "I trust the children I look after," she said. "They seem to know that."

That's when we moved on to the topic of the trust that exists between children and their parents, and how threatening a divorce must be to a child's feelings of trust and also of love. From a child's point of view, did the breakdown of trust and love between husband and wife have to result in the same breakdowns between the child and his or her mother and father? It certainly might be natural for the child to assume so, and how sad and frightening that assumption would be! It might lead to the child's attempt to use someone else outside the family as a source of that trust and love.

"Come to think of it, that's just what I wanted to let Nat know," Nancy said at this point. "I wanted him to know he could trust me even if he didn't feel he could trust his folks. I wanted him to feel he could trust someone."

"It sounds like he sure does trust you, and that's got to be important for him. But I guess there's a difference between his trusting you instead of his parents or in addition to his parents."

She thought that over for a moment and then said vehemently, "Well, there's one thing I've decided, and that's if Mrs. Lynch calls again to change plans, she can tell the kids herself. I'm not going to get in the middle like I did that time. They can work it out themselves. But what am I going to do about Nat wanting to run away? Should I tell his mom?"

"First, why don't you see if Nat wants to talk some more about it," I suggested. "I'll bet he didn't really want to run away at all. My guess is that what he wanted was to find out if anyone still loved him enough to stop him. You did. Maybe that's all he needed.

"But, Nancy, I do think this: If you get really worried about it, you *should* tell Mrs. Lynch. Sometimes adults have to make decisions like that out of genuine concern and caring for children. It's hard, but I don't think we need to feel guilty about it."

I had the sense that our talk gave Nancy some relief. It seemed to let her lift some responsibility off her own shoulders and put it back where it rightfully belonged.

That evening I went over to Montefiore Hospital and dropped in on Ruth Lynch. On my way to her room, I stopped at the nurses' station and was assured that she was doing just fine. And, lying there in her bed, Ruth did look like her old self.

"What a nice surprise!" she said. "Who on earth told you I was vacationing here?"

I let her know that I'd seen Karen and Virginia and that I wished I could've gotten here sooner.

"Oh, I've had lots of visitors, Will—not, mind you, that you aren't especially welcome. Everyone's been treating me like the Queen of Sheba. It's not often that a farm girl gets to put her feet up like this. But they sure don't leave you in peace for much at a time . . . all that poking and prodding! And I'd say the cook could do with a couple of my recipes."

"How long are they going to keep you here?"

"No time at all. Just long enough to make sure everything's ticking along okay. Which, I'm glad to say, it seems to be."

She went on matter-of-factly to tell me that she thought she'd been having indigestion and hadn't thought much about it until she'd started getting a pain in her arm and feeling dizzy. "Of course, when I plumb passed out it scared the wits out of Dwight. We had an ambulance and everything. My oh my, what a commotion!"

"You're going to take it easy now, I hope."

"Well, I'm going to be sensible, if that's what you mean . . . lose some of this padding." She patted the sheet over her stomach. "Maybe I'll let Dwight take over in the kitchen. My trouble is, I like my own cooking."

"You'd better not let him start in until after Christmas, Ruth, or you're going to have a lot of disappointed people."

She laughed. "No, I reckon I'll have to get us through the holidays, all right. Mind you, I don't know how that'll all work out this year. But I suppose everyone's going to get out to the farm sooner or later."

"It won't be the same, will it?"

"Nope. It won't be the same. That seems to be the way the world works these days, and there's no use spending a lot of time grumbling about things you can't do anything about. People have got to lead their own lives. Sometimes what you want for them doesn't turn out to be what they want for themselves. Sure is hard to let go, though. Seems like things were easier for families in the old days, but I don't suppose they were. Just different."

"I wonder about that, too," I said. "Did you grow up on a farm?"

"Oh, yes. My daddy had a little farm here in western Pennsylvania . . . not much of a place, but sufficient to feed and raise a family. Of course, we missed out on a lot of the things kids get these days—a good education, what they call 'culture,' and all that. But it was a healthy life for kids. Seemed hard sometimes. There were always chores to do just when you wanted to go play, and it could get mighty cold walking to school in the winter. But we sure had our place in the scheme of things.

"I guess that's not something that seems important 'til you get a lot older," she went on, "but a person can't get by without knowing where he's at. Growing up, we never had time to wonder what we were good for. Mother Nature made sure of that. Take Nat and Sharon, now. They don't scarcely know where they belong or maybe even who they belong to. Why, it must seem to them that there's nothing and no one to be trusted anymore. That Sharon—she's a real bright little devil—got to asking me all about *promises* the last time we saw each other."

"Promises?"

"Oh, she's always full of questions! But that day she really had something on her mind."

* * *

"Those kids sure can put away your gingerbread!" Dwight Lynch said, coming into the living room. "So could I, for that matter."

Ruth, in the rocking chair, looked up from her sewing. "They can't have eaten it *all*!"

"No, but at least half. And you made one heck of a lot." He picked up the morning paper, let himself down into the overstuffed chair with a grunt, and started reading where he had left off earlier in the day. "More snow forecast," he commented.

It's so good for him to have the children here, she thought. He gets out and does things he doesn't do otherwise. In fact, he does more things than he used to do with Fred and Gloria when they were small. Of course, he's got the time nowadays. Back then it always seemed like he was too busy. Maybe that was part of the problem. Fred's such a good boy, but he's always been so . . . so uncertain about himself. I guess we spoiled our kids some, too, come to think of it.

"Nathan ever ask you about coming to live with us?" Dwight suddenly asked, lowering his paper.

"No," she replied. "Why?"

"He's mentioned it to me a couple of times since summer."

"I hope you told him he'd always be welcome."

"Well, no, I didn't. At least not like that. I tried to tell him that all kids need parents as well as grandparents."

Ruth stopped her work. "Nobody needs to be pulled apart *between* parents, though. Just look at Christmas this year! Fred will be here, Karen will be in her house, her folks are clear across town, and Nat and Sharon will spend most of the time in someone's car shuttling back and forth to keep the grown-ups happy. I think it would be just dandy for the kids to be *here*—and let the grown-ups come and go as they please! Have you even thought about who's supposed to give who presents, and where, and when? I tell you!"

Dwight was leaning back in the chair now, his eyes closed and the newspaper in a heap on the floor. He shook his head. "Uh-uh. So long as there's no emergency, it's best for them all to work it out. It's tough, I grant you. But so's life. We raised our kids the best we could, and now it's their turn. We're here if they need us."

She thought about that for a while as she went on with her sewing. She could hear Nathan and Sharon crayoning at the kitchen table—the occasional scrape of a chair on the linoleum floor; little altercations over whose turn it was to use which color; disagreements over what something was meant to look like; but, all in all, surprisingly peaceful. I think we'd be very happy together for a while, she thought. We could give things a kind of center, what with Fred uncertain about his future and Karen talking about going back to school. Well, you can bet *she* won't stay single for long, and then she'll probably move and take the children with her.

"You watch," she said aloud. "We're going to lose contact with them. Karen will remarry, and then we won't see them at all."

Dwight made no response, but she had expected none, knowing that he was off on one of his frequent catnaps.

Later, Nat appeared in the doorway between the kitchen and the living room. "Is it half an hour yet, Nana?" he asked.

"Must be pretty near. Did Gramps say to wake him up?"

"Uh-huh."

"Well, I'm awake already," Dwight said, clearing his throat and blinking his eyes into focus. "Always got to sleep with one eye open in case the fox gets into the chicken coop."

"What've you two got planned?" Ruth asked.

"We're going to look at the decorations in the store windows! C'mon, Gramps," Nat said, "let's go!"

As the two pulled on their coats and boots and left, laughing, Sharon came into the room.

"What are you sewing, Nana?" she wanted to know.

"Why, that's your brother's Cub Scout uniform. Didn't you want to go with Nat and Gramps?"

Sharon was hanging onto the arm of the sofa, swinging one leg back and forth. "No. Why are you doing it?"

"I promised Nat I'd sew his new badges on, and they have to be in the right places or he can't wear it. They can't be crooked either."

"How do you know where they go?"

"He showed me."

"Can't Mommy sew them?"

"She's busy, so I told her I'd do it. And I told Nat I'd have it finished by the time he and Gramps got back."

"What happens if you don't?"

"Well, he needs it for tomorrow, and I guess your mommy would have to finish it up tonight. But I don't like saying I'll do something and then not doing it."

Sharon clambered onto the couch and slumped against the cushions at the back. "What's a promise?"

Ruth took a couple of pins out of her mouth and thought for a minute. "Well . . . it's telling someone you'll do something . . . and really *meaning* it. Saying you 'promise' to do something makes it more important."

"And if you don't do it?"

"That's a *broken* promise. It's bad to break promises."

"Like when Mommy tells me she's coming home before I go to bed and she doesn't."

"Does she *promise* she will?"

Sharon nodded.

Ruth put down her sewing. "You know, Sharon, there are times when people really can't help breaking promises. Or changing them, let's say. The car might not start just when they need it. Or they might get sick. Or something like that."

"Mommy went to a movie."

In spite of herself, Ruth felt a twinge of irritation. This is like getting the third degree, or whatever they call it, she thought.

"Maybe she should ask you first if she has to change a promise. Would that make you feel better about it?"

Sharon nodded and slithered off the sofa onto the floor.

"Now look here," Ruth said. "I've got two more badges to do before I'm finished. See if you can find me another spool of blue thread in my sewing basket. Dark blue."

Sharon crawled over to the basket on the floor beside her grandmother's chair and rummaged around in it. "This one?" she asked, holding up a spool.

"That's the one. Thank you very much."

"Nana . . ."

"Mmmmm?"

"Did Daddy break a promise when he went away?"

Land sakes, she thought, what all is going on in your little head? "No," she said, "I wouldn't say that. It's more like your mother and father agreed to change their promise about living with each other."

Sharon said nothing, and Ruth let it go at that. She was aware, though, that there was far more to say. Yes, honey, she thought, there were also "promises" made about living with you and Nat, about being a family. . . .

"Since you're so interested in promises today, young lady," she said brightly, "how about your giving me one?"

"What?" Sharon asked.

"I want you to promise me that when you get home you'll ask your mother if you can come and live with us next summer for two whole weeks. How about that?"

Sharon edged up to her grandmother's chair and leaned her head against it.

"Well?"

When Sharon still said nothing, Ruth continued, "We could do all the fun things you like. Go to the park and the pool. Play with your friend, Cathy. I bet Granddad would even take you fishing. How about it?"

Sharon shook her head.

Perplexed, Ruth turned and looked at her granddaughter. "Why, Sharon Lynch!" she said. "Here I thought you liked coming to see us!"

Sharon nodded.

"Does that mean you do or you don't?" Ruth asked.

"I do," Sharon murmured.

"Well, then, what's this all about?"

"I just don't want to say any promises," Sharon said, verging on tears.

Ruth took her in her arms. "Oh, sweet pea, I didn't mean to upset you that way! Of course you don't have to promise anything! You know that Granddad and I are very happy whenever you and Nat come over. I'll talk to your mother about the summer myself. How about that?"

Sharon bobbed her head, relieved.

Holding her granddaughter tightly, Ruth began softly singing "When the Saints Go Marching In"—a song she had first sung to Sharon as a baby on her knee and one they had shared specially ever since. We've all got a long road ahead, she thought as she sang. Let's just hope it all comes out right in the end. . . .

"'Lord, I want to be in that number, when the stars begin to shine,'" she sang. Giving Sharon a kiss on the cheek, she said, "You just remember that you don't ever have to make a promise to anyone if you don't want to. Not to anyone!" Then she added, "I'd better get on with my promise to Nat, hadn't I? If I don't get this uniform finished, I'll be in trouble for sure!"

"Can we make some popcorn when you're done?"

"Sure we can. In fact, you know where I keep the pan and the corn. You go get the makings ready, and I'll be done in a jiffy!"

*   *   *

"Not easy to know what to tell kids," Ruth concluded.

"Or to know what they're asking sometimes."

She nodded and closed her eyes. Her face was soft and unwrinkled for her age, not at all one of those weather-beaten country faces. It was an indoor face, the face of a nurturer and provider. Even with her eyes closed, she wore an expression of patience and endurance. In that expression, though, there was no feeling of repose. Her eyes opened, meeting mine.

"I'm frightened, Will," she said.

"Of dying?" I asked gently.

"Of dying right now," she replied. "I know something now I didn't know before. You've got to be strong to die, and that strength is something you borrow from the people you love. No one seems to have got any to lend me."

"Not Dwight?"

"He's all at sixes and sevens. Oh, he's not falling apart or anything, not that man. But I guess we've never talked about one of us dying. A person needs to do that.

"Gloria and Fred have been in to see me. She just goes on telling me I'll be fine before I know it. Maybe she's right, and maybe she's not, but death isn't something she wants to look at. Fred's been good, but I know how hard it is for him to deal with one more worry, one more woe. The kids can't come because they're too young. I just want to live long enough to see them be all right."

"I hope you will, too, Ruth," I said. "I know it will be easier for them if you're there for them to count on."

"Dwight's right, you know. I keep thinking they ought to come live with us for a time, but he pooh-poohs the idea and asks why on earth I want to start mothering them when they've got a perfectly good mother of their own. So I guess I should just let them be."

"I can't think of anything more natural than your wanting to give them a happy home. But Karen is a good mother, and Fred's a good father. The kids need to know it. *And* to know that everyone still loves them a whole lot. A grandparent's house could be a mighty good place to hear all of that."

"Maybe they will," she said, and then added, "G-W-W-P."

"What's that mean?" I asked.

"It's something my granddad used to say when we'd pester him to promise we could do something, like ride in the buggy or help him chop ice or tap the maples. Funny," she said, "I haven't thought of that in years. He'd finally say, 'All right! All right! I promise we'll do it together ... G-W-W-P.' God Willing and Weather Permitting is what it stood for. Come to think of it, that's a pretty smart way to end any promise."

"Sure is," I agreed.

"In fact, you might just want to tuck it in the marriage service after the 'I do.'"

I laughed, but I somehow knew then that I'd never perform another marriage service without having a little voice in my head say exactly that.

I rose to leave. "I've got a parishioner up on five to visit," I said. "You take good care of yourself now, and do what they tell you."

"Oh, I reckon I'm their best patient. Meek as a lamb."

"I'll be over here again next week and look in on you then."

"Thanks, Will, for coming. But unless you've got other business here, you'd better call ahead next time. I'm sure not going to promise to sit around waiting for you."

"If I find an empty bed, that will be the best visit of all," I said, waving to her from the door. As it turned out, that was just what I did find.

# EPILOGUE

The turn of the year brought several changes in the lives of the Lynches and the Sawyers. One Sunday in January, Virginia Sawyer came up to me after church and told me that Karen was moving to Cincinnati in the spring. She was going to work full time at the Cincinnati Institute of Art until the fall and then start a Master's program in Art History at the University of Cincinnati. On that same Sunday, Virginia asked me if I would perform her niece's wedding the following April.

Fred was accepted at the State Police Academy in February. I'd been in touch with him two or three times since our meeting in September—short, friendly phone calls that told me he was having his predictable ups and downs but was coping fine. When he told me he was moving, I asked if he needed a hand, and on the Saturday of his departure for Hershey I went over to his apartment.

It was a very upbeat afternoon. Jack Geary and Gloria were there, as well as a fellow policeman, and together we were able to finish the packing and load up the rented truck in under three hours. Fred was to drive the truck, Jack was taking Fred's car, and Fred's other friend was going along, too, in his own car, to bring Jack back on the following evening. Gloria and I waved the convoy off at around 5:30, and then she asked me back to her house for supper.

There I learned that everything was fine out at the farm. Ruth was being careful but doing well and working hard at her weight problem. I talked to Ruth not long after that and told her I'd come out in the spring when the trees were in flower. G-W-W-P.

I see Nancy all the time. I think she's in love, but she hasn't said anything about it to me and I haven't asked. If it's who I think it is, she's going to have her hands full.

Karen's remark about not attending church because she felt she would be judged struck home with me. I'm glad we're family-oriented in the church, but Karen made me see how oriented we are toward intact and tidy families. Just as children need to hear that divorced husbands and wives don't stop being mothers and fathers, so those of us in the church need that reminder, too. During the last few months I've encouraged my divorced parishioners— parents and non-parents alike—to get together here at Sixth Church and support one another. Several have told me they have found this helpful.

I saw Karen only once before she left for Cincinnati, and that was at her cousin's wedding in April. The wedding was a very swell affair, with Nat as ringbearer and Sharon as flower girl. The bride wore an heirloom wedding dress, and I'd never seen Sixth Church more colorfully bedecked in spring bouquets and floods of sunlight.

I had a lot of trouble writing a prayer for the occasion. I managed to start off well: *Teach them how to love one another, O Lord, with all the fullness of life you have given us. Enable them to use their times of anger. . . .* And that's where I got stuck, again and again. I wanted a prayer that would be realistic and not just full of pious platitudes. We don't talk about anger in church, and we should. What I really wanted to come up with was a prayer that would have enough zing to carry this couple through to the end, through all the rough spots. I wanted to give them something to hold onto in a storm. If only that were possible, ever!

*Enable them to use their times of anger. . . .* Use them for what? There is such a thing as a good fight. More couples should have them. Should I pray that they fight well? The bride's mother would have a fit! How about praying that the two of them be open and honest with their anger? Not hide it? Use it to grow even closer in their marriage? *Enable them to use their times of anger openly and honestly and for healing,* I tried. That seemed to break my mental block, and here is what I finally wrote:

Eternal God, you have heard the promises Peter and Laurie have made to one another. It's their first step in marriage. We pray that each day may unfold with new confidence and understanding for their journey. Teach them how to love one another with all the fullness of life you have given us. Enable them to use their times of anger openly and honestly and for healing. Help them to learn from the past and not be bound by it. Help them to find within their marriage the occasion for hope. Extend their relationship so that it may include others in the circle of their love. We pray for their parents. Confirm their pride. Help them to say goodbye to these children with a sense of trust in them and with the assurance that a new relationship is about to begin. We pray for us all. Encircle us with your love in all of our relationships. Amen.

It made me feel very good when, at the Country Club reception afterwards, Virginia made a point of telling me how much she had appreciated that prayer. I told her honestly that my being part of her "extended family" had helped me to write it.

It's chiefly through Virginia nowadays that I keep up with news of Nat and Sharon. Virginia comes to Sixth Church most Sundays, even though I've tried to let her know that I wouldn't take it personally if she went to a church closer to home. But she insists that she's comfortable with us here and that she's made some new friends she feels close to.

She's pleased with the way her grandchildren have started getting into their new lives, and she's been out to Cincinnati to visit them and help furnish and decorate the new house. She wishes the children could have their own rooms, but they seem to like bunk beds. She's seen their schools and has a lot of confidence in Karen's usual babysitter. It's clear that Virginia still feels very much a part of their lives—and vice versa.

We don't talk much about some of the harder feelings, but I think she would if she needed or wanted to. She did mention something, though, that said a whole lot: "I feel I'm finally learning to let go," she admitted, "and much to my surprise, everyone is still upright and moving along—me included." What an expression of growth!

I'm very aware that my own growth continues through every relationship I form. It seems to me that self-awareness and self-fulfillment in any human being are best nurtured through contacts with others of our species. Maybe that's what anthropologists and sociologists mean when they say that human beings are social animals. If that's true, though, why do we often have so much trouble "socializing"? I feel a sermon coming on about the difference between having a strong sense of self and being selfish, but I'll save that for another day.

Should I ever again get so involved in other family upsets as I did with the Lynches and Sawyers—and I probably will because it comes with the territory—I'll feel better prepared. Each will be different, of course, but anger and grief, guilt and disappointment will probably be common to them all. In everything that I see and do, those particular feelings come back again and again like old, familiar adversaries. It helps when you recognize them and acknowledge them. Even that seems to rob them of some of their potency.

Feelings, feelings, feelings: That's what the whole year was about to those people, parents and grandparents and children alike. They were awash in feelings. But aren't we all like that at times? Some feelings we confuse with others; some we simply deny because they make us uncomfortable . . . and that goes for the feelings other people have that make us uncomfortable, too. How easy it is to say, "Don't be upset," or "Don't cry," or "Don't be angry." Admonitions like that aren't much help, though.

Just the other day, I was confronted by an irate parishioner who gave me an earful about his adolescent son's latest escapade. I could feel my own anxiety mounting along with his anger. I wanted to cut him short, to say something like, "Don't take it so hard, Al! It happens to everyone." But I didn't. In the nick of time, I realized that such a response would have been more help to me than to him. Instead I said, "These are tough years, aren't they, Al? I can understand why you're outraged." His anger changed after that. Oh, he was still mad as hell, but he was less defensive and hostile.

It didn't occur to me then, but I wonder if he, like Dwight Lynch, felt as if his son's actions were all his fault as a parent. I wonder if he felt guilty about his anger and afraid I'd tell him that both he and his feelings were wrong. How can feelings be *wrong*? We feel what we feel, and we have our reasons. How we express those feelings . . . well, that's an entirely different matter.

Yes, I'm learning, I think. During this past year, I learned a lot about listening, for instance, and what a useful tool it can be for helping people sort out their feelings. More than that, concerned listening is likely to suggest that you value what someone is saying. That, in turn, is likely to suggest that you value the person who is doing the talking. And that's important.

Anger, guilt, and misery are usually accompanied—or caused—by the loss of self-worth. A little voice inside says, "I'm no longer someone worth listening to" or "No one cares enough about me to listen." Confirming and supporting a person's sense of self. . . . That seems to me to be the single most helpful thing we can do when a friend is in trouble. Letting a friend know that he or she is still a valued friend, or letting a loved one know that he or she is still lovable, is at the very root of helpfulness— and perhaps at the root of a person's ability to cope. How can self-help be found within a shattered self?

*Self*-help. Yes, that's been another lesson for me. I could have said the words before this year began and known that they were important. I could have quoted, "Give a man a fish and he will eat for a day. Teach a man to fish and he will eat for a lifetime." But until now their meaning would not have been part of me and my gut understanding of what real helpfulness is. I would not have understood that my urge to find solutions for other people's problems was in large part due to my own urgent need to feel helpful— or, in other words, to find a solution to *my* problem rather than theirs.

Even when one makes a small emotional investment in a human conflict, it's easy to take sides, to argue the rights and wrongs, to exonerate and to condemn. I doubt that those kinds of judgments, though, are components of either true friendship or true helpfulness, or that they qualify as "speaking truth in the spirit of love." Those of us on the edge of the conflict should, at least in theory, find it easier to remain nonjudgmental. Certainly it was a very different thing for me to want to be helpful than it was for Virginia Sawyer, say, or Gloria Houck or the Gearys. It was probably difficult for many of those people to even *want* to be helpful to one another. They all had their own powerful needs standing between them and genuine helpfulness.

No one can manage his or her feelings all the time, that's certain. There may be many occasions when our feelings render us incapable of giving the kinds of help other people most need. Perhaps all we can try to do at times like that is to keep ourselves from using our feelings in destructive or vengeful ways. That would be very helpful in itself.

There was no one I spoke to in or around this particular divorce who would not have wanted to be truly helpful to the children—to Nat and Sharon. Most everyone was uncertain about what to do, but they all wanted to do something. In my mind, there are two things we can do for children caught in a divorce: We can help them learn that they are not the cause of the breakup, and we can try to strengthen their sense of continuing love from their parents, relatives, and friends.

Why is it, I wonder, that some kids who seem to have the odds stacked against them manage to thrive all the same? I don't just mean kids from broken homes, but also kids who grow up in poverty and squalor amidst prejudice and abuse and danger. Some still make it and become whole and fulfilled adult human beings. What's the reason? Genetics? Or love?

I'll put my money on love. I'd bet that somewhere along the way, despite the odds, those children found someone who truly loved them, someone who let them know that they were lovable for who they were. Armed with that knowledge, even the children of trauma stand a good chance of growing into loving adults.

May we all aspire to be that someone in the lives of others. May we be there for them when they need us. And may we all be fortunate enough to find that someone when we, ourselves, are in need.

Amen, oh Lord, amen!

*Scenes from a Divorce* was written under a grant to Family Communications, Inc., from Lilly Endowment, Inc., as part of the *Let's Talk about It*® series. *Let's Talk about It*® materials are designed to encourage communication between children and adults. Additional materials have been developed on: pets, discipline, creativity, day care, going to the hospital, visiting the dentist, starting school, moving to a new home, and experiencing a death in the family. For more information, write to: Family Communications, 4802 Fifth Ave., Pittsburgh, Pennsylvania 15213.